St Oswald's Way

OFFICIAL GUIDE BOOK

St. Oswald's Way – Official Guidebook
First edition published in 2007 by Alnwick District Council
Copyright Northumberland County Council

This guidebook, copyright (2024) was written or edited by Martin Paminter
of the St. Oswald's Way Management Group.

Published by:
Northern Heritage Services Ltd, Blagdon Estate, Northumberland, NE13 6DB
on behalf of St. Oswald's Way Management Group.
ISBN: 9781739486136

Mapping contains data from OS Crown copyright and database right 2024
and OpenStreetMap contributors, Openstreetmap.org/copyright.
Cartography by Richard Ross, Active Maps Ltd.

Printed and bound in the UK by Latitude Press

A catalogue record of this book is available from the British Library.

All rights reserved.
No part of this book maybe reproduced, stored or introduced into a retrieval system, or transmitted in any form or by any means (electronic, mechanical, photocopying, recording or otherwise) without the prior permission of the publisher, except in the case of brief quotations embodied in critical reviews and certain other non-commercial uses permitted by copyright law.

INDEX

Introduction

4 .... St Oswald's Way

5 .... St Oswald's Way Overview Map

6 .... How to use this Book

6 .... St. Oswald's Way Certificates

7-8 .... A Short History of Oswald

Information and Advice

9 .... Preparation for Your Walk

10 .... The Countryside Code

11 .... Walking on Roads

11 .... Golf Courses

13 .... Other Long-Distance Walks in the Area

14-15...... Waymarking and Signage

16-17...... Public Transport

18 .... Car Parking

18 .... Accommodation and Tourist Information

19 .... Facilities En Route

20-21 ..... St Oswald's Way Route Distance Table

22 .... Map of Whole Route

23 .... Key to Maps

Walk Sections

24-35 ..... **Section 1** - Holy Island to Bamburgh

36-47...... **Section 2** - Bamburgh to Craster

48-59 ..... **Section 3** - Craster to Warkworth

60-73 ..... **Section 4** - Warkworth to Rothbury

74-87 ..... **Section 5** - Rothbury to Kirkwhelpington

88-101 ... **Section 6** - Kirkwhelpington to Heavenfield

102 .... **Link Route** - Heavenfield to Wall/Hexham

103 .... Merchandise

104 .... Useful Websites
Acknowledgements

ST. OSWALD'S WAY

St. Oswald's Way is a long-distance walking route, exploring some of the finest landscapes and fascinating history of Northumberland, England's northernmost county.

You will find castles, coastline, islands, scenic river valleys, hills, attractive villages, forest and farmland on your walk.

From Holy Island (Lindisfarne) in the north, St. Oswald's Way follows the stunning Northumberland coast, before heading inland across beautiful countryside to Hadrian's Wall and Heavenfield in the south, a distance of 96 miles (155km).

The route links some of the places associated with St. Oswald, the king of Northumbria in the early 7th century, who played a major part in bringing Christianity to his people. It is based on a walk devised by Embleton Church Council and implemented in a project led by Alnwick District Council. It was launched in 2006.

Nowadays, the route is supported by the St Oswald's Way Management Group. The Management Group is responsible for the overall management of the path, including the production of the official guidebook, maintenance of the website, issuing certificates, publicity and liaison with Northumberland County Council. They also have a team of volunteer rangers who monitor the condition of the paths on a regular basis and carry out minor maintenance, alongside more major work carried out by the County Council, Northumberland National Park and land managers.

Profits from the sale of this book and other merchandise will provide support to the St Oswald's Way Management Group and help them to ensure the future of the route.

SOW managers and volunteers

ROUTE OVERVIEW

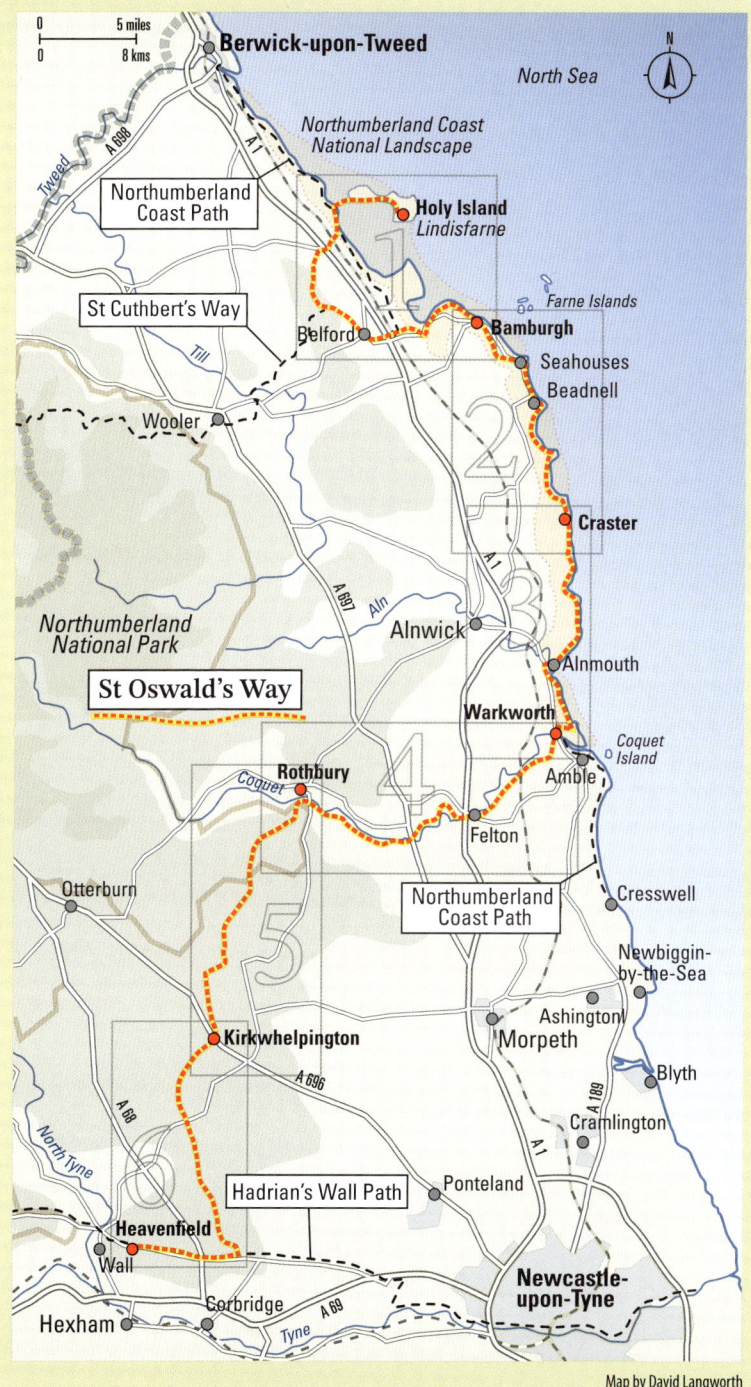

Map by David Langworth

HOW TO USE THIS BOOK

This St. Oswald's Way Official Guidebook is full of useful information to make your walk as enjoyable as possible. General information and advice for the walker is included in the early part of the book, followed by the details of the route.

St. Oswald's Way is divided into six sections, from north to south:

1. Holy Island to Bamburgh (19 miles / 30 km)
2. Bamburgh to Craster (14 miles / 23 km)
3. Craster to Warkworth (13 miles / 21 km)
4. Warkworth to Rothbury (18 miles / 29 km)
5. Rothbury to Kirkwhelpington (15 miles / 24 km)
6. Kirkwhelpington to Heavenfield (17 miles / 28 km)

You can, of course, walk the route in different sections, or even in the opposite direction, but please be aware that the book is written 'from north to south'.

Each section of St. Oswald's Way has its own chapter, with detailed maps and a route description to help you find your way. There is also information on the many interesting places and features to be found, and numerous photographs of the beautiful views and historic sites than can be seen.

For those wishing to find out more about Northumberland, what to do, where to stay and how to get around, the final part of the book gives contact details for a number of organisations that will be pleased to help.

ST. OSWALD'S WAY CERTIFICATES

If you have walked the whole length of St. Oswald's Way, you will be able to receive a commemorative certificate.

As you follow the route, you will be able to find six St. Oswald's Way interpretation panels. The panels can be found at Holy Island, Bamburgh, Warkworth, Rothbury, Kirkwhelpington and Heavenfield and you will need to show that you have visited each one.

Details of the how to find the panels and the evidence you need to collect can be found on the St. Oswald's Way website.

A SHORT HISTORY OF OSWALD

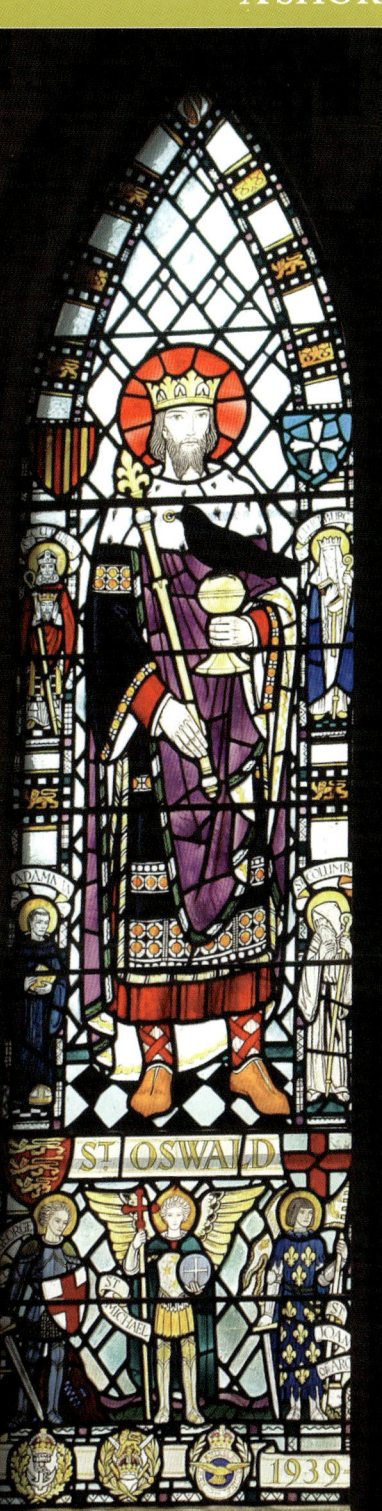

St. Oswald's Way links three important sites associated with the Northumbrian king and saint, Oswald. These are the Holy Island of Lindisfarne, where he installed the first bishop; Bamburgh, which was his royal capital, and Heavenfield, where he won the famous battle that made him king.

Oswald was born in about 605 and was killed in 642. What is known of his life and achievements is almost entirely dependent on the *'Ecclesiastical History of the English People'* written by the North East historian and scholar, the Venerable Bede, in about 730. This was some 90 years after Oswald's death. Bede portrays Oswald as a "man beloved of God" and the ideal Christian king – in life and death fighting for Christianity.

Oswald was the son of Aethelfrith, the King of Bernicia. Aethelfrith's wife, Acha, was from the royal family of the neighbouring kingdom of Deira, which allowed him to 'England' north of the Humber. her, Edwin, in 616 and Acha, Oswald and other companions fled to Dal Riada, in what is now Scotland. While he was there, Oswald was converted to Christianity by monks from the island of Iona.

Meanwhile Edwin's reign brought peace and prosperity to Northumbria and he expanded his area of power westwards. However, in 633 he was killed in a battle against Cadwallon, the King of Gwynedd, and Penda of Mercia. Oswald's elder step-brother was king for a short period, until he was also killed by Cadwallon, who took a terrible revenge for the defeats of his people in earlier years.

Oswald had returned from exile when Edwin was killed and he marched south from his headquarters at Bamburgh to Heavenfield in order to confront Cadwallon. Before the victorious battle, Oswald set up the standard of the holy cross before which, Bede says, "as far as we know, there was no symbol of the Christian faith, no church, and no altar erected anywhere in the land of Bernicia".

Shortly after becoming king, Oswald asked Iona for a spiritual leader to help in the conversion of Northumbria to Christianity. The first candidate was of "austere disposition" and soon returned to Iona. He was replaced by Aidan, who was given the island of Lindisfarne by Oswald for his base. Aidan was made Bishop of Lindisfarne in 635 and the island went on to become the cradle of Christianity in England.

Oswald ruled Northumbria for eight years and his reign ushered in a golden period in Northumbrian history in which scholarship, art and building flourished. It lasted until the Viking raids began in 793.

King Oswald was one of the most important rulers in Britain, but was killed in battle at Maserfield (thought to be near Oswestry in Shropshire), fighting his old enemies from Gwynedd and Mercia. After his death, his body was hacked to pieces and the head and arms fixed to stakes on the orders of Penda.

In the following year, Oswald's head and arms were rescued by his brother, Oswiu. The arms were taken to Bamburgh and, according to one source, Oswiu built the church of St. Peter at Bamburgh to house them. The head was given to the Lindisfarne Monastery, where it remained until Viking raids forced the monks to flee the island in the 9th century. The head was one of the treasures, which also included the body of St. Cuthbert, that they took with them. Oswald's head is now in St. Cuthbert's tomb in Durham Cathedral.

All these relics and the sites of Heavenfield and Maserfield became associated with miracles – and miraculous cures. These stories and the records of Bede were the beginnings of a cult of St. Oswald and his life became the inspiration for legends as the cult spread throughout Europe in the Middle Ages. Stories and images of Oswald developed, in which a raven was shown as his companion and messenger. The raven is now used as the symbol for St. Oswald's Way.

INFORMATION AND ADVICE

PREPARATION FOR YOUR WALK

Before setting off on your walk along St. Oswald's Way, check the weather forecast and prepare yourself accordingly. Remember that weather conditions can change quickly at any time of year. Parts of the route cross remote countryside where it is always worth having proper walking boots and a set of good waterproofs with you, along with a first aid kit and enough food and drink. On the hills, it may also be worth taking a GPS-enabled device or compass with you to help navigation, especially in poor weather.

The route of St Oswald's Way is subject to temporary and permanent diversions. It will be important to check the website: **www.stoswaldsway.com** for changes to the route from the one described in this guidebook. GPX files of the up-to-date route are also available on the website.

North of Low Newton

INFORMATION AND ADVICE

The Countryside Code

Respect other people
- Consider the local community and other people enjoying the outdoors
- Park carefully so access to gateways and driveways is clear
- Leave gates and property as you find them
- Follow paths but give way to others where it's narrow

Protect the natural environment
- Leave no trace of your visit, take all your litter home
- Don't have BBQs or fires
- Keep dogs under effective control
- Dog poo - bag it and bin it

Enjoy the outdoors
- Plan ahead, check what facilities are open, be prepared
- Follow advice and local signs and obey social distancing measures

Enjoy, be safe

INFORMATION AND ADVICE

WALKING ON ROADS

Although most of St. Oswald's Way follows public rights of way and other paths, there are numerous sections where country roads must be used. Please take great care when walking along roads and remember to follow the Highway Code:

- **Pavements or paths** should be used if provided.

- **If there is no pavement or path**, walk on the right-hand side of the road so that you can see oncoming traffic. You should take extra care and;

be prepared to walk in single file, especially on narrow roads or in poor light,

keep close to the side of the road.

It is often safer to cross the road well before a sharp right-hand bend (so that oncoming traffic has a better chance of seeing you). Cross back after the bend.

- **Help other road users to see you.** Wear or carry something light coloured, bright or fluorescent in poor daylight conditions.

If you are a **large group** of people, you should use a path or pavement if available; if one is not, you should keep to the left. Look-outs should be positioned at the front and back of the group, and they should wear fluorescent clothes in daylight and reflective clothes in the dark.

GOLF COURSES

The northern part of St. Oswald's Way crosses or runs alongside golf courses in a number of places. When walking through these areas, please follow the waymarks and do not stray from the path. Be aware of golfers and watch out for flying golf balls. It is not always easy to tell where the balls will be coming from, so keep a constant look-out as you walk.

INFORMATION AND ADVICE

St. Aidan's Dunes

INFORMATION AND ADVICE

OTHER LONG-DISTANCE WALKS IN THE AREA

St. Oswald's Way shares parts of the routes of other promoted walks that cross Northumberland.

St. Cuthbert's Way links a number of places associated with the former Bishop of Lindisfarne. It runs from Melrose Abbey in the Scottish Borders, crosses the rugged Cheviot Hills, then passes through Wooler and on to end at Holy Island. The route is 62 miles (100 km) in length.

The **Northumberland Coast Path** is part of the North Sea Trail project. The Northumberland section of this pan-European route runs from Cresswell up to Berwick-upon-Tweed. It includes the whole length of the Northumberland Coast Area of Outstanding Natural Beauty. The Path is 62 miles (100 km) long.

The King Charles III **England Coast Path** is a new National Trail around the whole English coast. It is the longest managed coastal path in the world and is approximately 2,700 miles (4,300 km) in total.

Hadrian's Wall Path is an 84-miles (135 km) coast-to-coast National Trail along the famous Roman frontier, from Wallsend in the east to Bowness-on-Solway in the west. It passes through some beautiful countryside, from rolling fields to rugged moorland, and includes the cities of Newcastle-upon-Tyne and Carlisle.

The **Northern Saints Trails** are a set of six long-distance walks, rooted in the North East's Christian heritage. Two of them connect with St. Oswald's Way at Warkworth and Heavenfield.

INFORMATION AND ADVICE

WAYMARKING AND SIGNAGE

St. Oswald's Way is, in parts, shared with other promoted walking routes that cross Northumberland. Although the route is waymarked and signed, we have tried to avoid cluttering the countryside with too many arrows and signs. There is, therefore, a variety of waymarking to follow as you progress along your walk.

Public footpaths (yellow arrows) and public bridleways (blue arrows) are followed for most of St. Oswald's Way. Follow the waymarking for these paths where appropriate, and look out for the additional waymarks and signs for the promoted routes.

The first part of St. Oswald's Way (SOW), from Lindisfarne Priory on Holy Island to the mainland, is shared with St. Cuthbert's Way and the England Coast Path (ECP) but is little waymarked. At the end of the Holy Island Causeway, the three routes join the Northumberland Coast Path (NCP). The four routes run together briefly, before the ECP heads southwards.

For the next few miles, the route is waymarked with the distinctive discs and signs for the NCP (featuring the symbol for the North Sea Trail) with joint waymark discs for SOW and NCP, along with some St. Cuthbert's Way signs too.

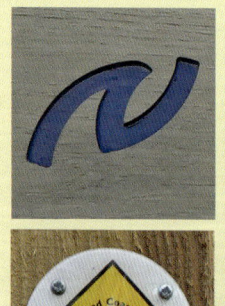

St. Cuthbert's Way heads off west via St. Cuthbert's Cave towards Wooler, while St. Oswald's Way and the NCP

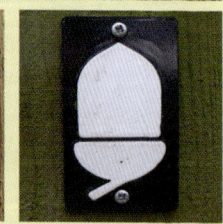

INFORMATION AND ADVICE

head south together. They rejoin the ECP on the eastern side of Belford. The ECP is one of England's family of National Trails and is marked with the distinctive 'acorn' logo used on all the National Trails.

The three routes run together until Bamburgh (Sections 1 and 2), where SOW and NCP take an inland route before rejoining the ECP to the north of Seahouses. All three routes then stay together as far as Warkworth (end of Section 3).

The Coast Paths continue southwards down the coast from Warkworth, but St. Oswald's Way heads west along the Coquet valley (Section 4). From Warkworth you will see waymarks, logos and signposts for St. Oswald's Way, until beyond Great Whittington in Section 6.

The last part of Section 6 is shared with Hadrian's Wall Path, another National Trail, as it makes its way from east to west.

The final few miles of St. Oswald's Way are, therefore, marked with the 'acorn' symbol.

To help you, the maps in this book make clear which routes are shared in which sections.

INFORMATION AND ADVICE

PUBLIC TRANSPORT

Most parts of St. Oswald's Way can be reached easily by public transport. Using buses and trains is better for the environment than travelling by car, and you will also be helping to retain these services that are vital to many people in rural areas. If you can't get to both ends of your walk by public transport, why not try using a bus or train in one direction and walking in the opposite direction?

Section 1 – Holy Island to Bamburgh

An irregular bus service runs between Holy Island and Berwick-upon-Tweed (where there is a railway station) also stopping on the A1 near Beal. Regular buses run along the A1, from Berwick, stopping near Beal, near Fenwick, Belford and southwards via Alnwick and Morpeth through to Newcastle upon Tyne. Other bus services run from Berwick and Belford, stopping at Waren Mill and Bamburgh, on their way to Alnwick.

Section 2 – Bamburgh to Craster

Regular bus services run between Berwick, Belford and along the coast to Alnwick, also stopping at Bamburgh, Seahouses, Beadnell, High Newton-by-the-Sea and Craster.

Section 3 – Craster to Warkworth

A regular bus service runs between Bamburgh and Alnwick, also stopping at Craster, Howick, Boulmer, Alnmouth railway station and Alnmouth village. Regular bus services run between Newcastle and Alnwick, including stops at Alnmouth village, Alnmouth railway station, Warkworth and Morpeth,

Alnmouth railway station lies about 1 mile to the west of the village and just ½ mile from St. Oswald's Way. Trains to and from Newcastle, Morpeth, Acklington, Berwick-upon-Tweed and Edinburgh can be used.

Section 4 – Warkworth to Rothbury

Warkworth can be easily reached by regular bus services to Alnwick, Morpeth and Newcastle. A different hourly bus service runs between Alnwick, Morpeth and Newcastle, stopping at Felton. A regular service also runs between Newcastle, Morpeth and Rothbury, stopping on the A697 at Weldon Bridge on the way. There are also direct buses between Rothbury and Alnwick.

INFORMATION AND ADVICE

Acklington railway station is 1 mile from St. Oswald's Way. Occasional local trains stop here en route from Newcastle and Morpeth to Alnmouth.

Section 5 – Rothbury to Kirkwhelpington
Public transport is fairly limited on this section of the walk. Rothbury can be easily reached by regular buses from Newcastle via Morpeth. Buses also run between Knowesgate, Kirkwhelpington and Newcastle.

Section 6 – Kirkwhelpington to Heavenfield
Public transport can be fairly limited on this section of the walk. Buses run between Kirkwhelpington, Ponteland and Newcastle. Great Whittington and Port Gate (at the junction of the A68 and B6318) can be both reached by buses to and from Newcastle, Ponteland and Hexham.

Unfortunately, there is no public transport to Heavenfield and no suitable car parking. You are advised to continue walking to either the village of Wall, or head south to Acomb or Hexham. Regular buses run between Wall, Acomb and Hexham. There are frequent buses between Hexham and Newcastle, along with a regular train service.

The detailed maps later on give a good indication of where you can catch buses and trains. Please be aware that routes are subject to change. For full and up-to-date route information and timetable details, contact: **Traveline using their app or web – website: travelinenortheast.info**

INFORMATION AND ADVICE

CAR PARKING

There are car parks in various places along St. Oswald's Way, as shown on the maps in this book – please use these car parks where possible. If parking at other places on the route, please make sure that you do not obstruct roads or gateways.

ACCOMMODATION AND TOURIST INFORMATION

There are guest houses and hotels at many places on the way, particularly along the coast (sections 1-3) and the Coquet valley (section 4). The countryside between Rothbury and Heavenfield, however, is quite remote and accommodation can be more difficult to find.

It is always advisable to book your accommodation, before you set out. Berwick-upon-Tweed Visitor Information Centre (see below for contact details) can help with advice on where to stay. You could also try **www.visitnorthumberland.com** where you can search for availability, as well as for general visitor information for the county.

Tourist and Visitor Information Centres

Berwick Library, Walkergate, Berwick-upon-Tweed, TD15 1DB
Tel: 01670 622155
Email: berwick.tic@northumberland.gov.uk

Seafield Road Car Park, Seahouses, NE68 7SW (seasonal only)
Tel: 01670 625593
Email: seahouses.tic@northumberland.gov.uk

Craster Car Park, Craster, NE66 3TW (seasonal only)
Tel: 01665 576007
Email: craster.tic@northumberland.gov.uk

The Chantry, Bridge Street, Morpeth, NE61 1PD
Tel: 01670 623455
Email: morpeth.tic@northumberland.gov.uk

Hill Street, Corbridge, NE45 5AA
Tel: 01434 632815
Email: corbridge.tic@northumberland.gov.uk

Hexham Library, Hexham, NE46 3LS
Tel: 01670 620450
Email: hexham.tic@northumberland.gov.uk

INFORMATION AND ADVICE

ST. OSWALD'S WAY - FACILITIES EN ROUTE

Location	Section	Bus	Train	Car Park	Toilets	Groceries	Pub	Rest/Cafe	Tourist Info
Holy Island	1	X		X	X	X	X	X	
A1 at Fenwick	1	X							
Fenwick	1						X		
Belford	1	X		X	X	X	X	X	
Waren Mill (Budle Bay)	1	X		X					
Bamburgh	1&2	X		X	X	X	X	X	
Seahouses	2	X		X	X	X	X	X	X
Beadnell	2	X				X	X	X	
Beadnell Harbour	2			X	X				
Newton Links House	2			X					
High Newton-by-the-Sea	2	X		X		X			
Low Newton-by-the-Sea	2			X	X	X			
Golf club (house)	2						X		
Embleton	2	X				X	X		
Dunstan Steads	2			X					
Craster	2&3	X		X	X	X	X	X	X
Nr Low Stead, Long'h'ton	3			X					
Boulmer	3	X		X	X	X			
Alnmouth	3	X		X	X	X	X	X	
Hipsburn	3	X	X	X					
Warkworth Dunes	3			X	X				
Warkworth	3&4	X		X	X	X	X	X	
Acklington (station)	4		X			X			
Felton / West Thirston	4	X				X	X	X	
Weldon Bridge	4	X				X			
Rothbury	4&5	X		X	X	X	X	X	
Lordenshaws	5			X					
Knowesgate	5	X					X		
Kirkwhelpington	5&6	X		X	X				
Great Whittington	6	X				X			
Port Gate / A68 round'b't	6							X	
Wall		X		X	X	X			
Acomb		X				X			
Hexham		X	X	X	X	X	X	X	X

INFORMATION AND ADVICE

ST. OSWALD'S WAY ROUTE DISTANCE TABLE

Section	Place	Distance from start of section		Distance from end of section		Distance from Lindisfarne Priory		Distance from Heavenfield	
		(miles)	(km)	(miles)	(km)	(miles)	(km)	(miles)	(km)
1	Lindisfarne Priory	0	0	18.5	29.8	0	0	96.0	154.5
1	Mainland (end of causeway)	3.6	5.8	14.9	24.1	3.6	5.8	92.5	148.8
1	Fenwick	5.8	9.4	12.7	20.4	5.8	9.4	90.2	145.2
1	Swinhoe Farm	10.3	16.7	8.2	13.2	10.3	16.7	85.7	137.9
1	Belford	12.2	19.6	6.3	10.2	12.2	19.6	83.9	134.9
1	Waren Mill	15.5	25.0	3.0	4.8	15.5	25.0	80.5	129.6
1	Bamburgh	18.5	29.8	0	0	18.5	29.8	77.5	124.7
2	Bamburgh	0	0	14.2	22.9	18.5	29.8	77.5	124.7
2	Seahouses	3.7	5.9	10.5	17.0	22.2	35.7	73.9	118.8
2	Beadnell	6.1	9.8	8.1	13.0	24.6	39.6	71.4	114.9
2	Beadnell Harbour car park	6.7	10.8	7.5	12.1	25.2	40.6	70.8	114.0
2	Newton Steads car park	8.8	14.1	5.4	8.8	27.3	43.9	68.8	110.6
2	Low Newton-by-the-Sea	10.4	16.7	3.8	6.1	28.9	46.6	67.1	108.0
2	Parking near Dunstan Steads	12.0	19.4	2.2	3.5	30.6	49.2	65.5	105.4
2	Craster	14.2	22.9	0	0	32.7	52.7	63.3	101.9
3	Craster	0	0	13.1	21.1	32.7	52.7	63.3	101.9
3	Boulmer	4.4	7.1	8.7	14.0	37.2	59.8	58.9	94.7
3	Seaton Point	5.7	9.2	7.4	12.0	38.4	61.8	57.6	92.7
3	Alnmouth	7.4	12.0	5.7	9.2	40.2	64.6	55.9	89.9
3	Warkworth Dunes picnic site	12.4	20.0	0.7	1.1	45.2	72.7	50.9	81.9
3	Warkworth	13.1	21.1	0	0	45.8	73.8	50.2	80.8

INFORMATION AND ADVICE

ST. OSWALD'S WAY ROUTE DISTANCE TABLE

Section	Place	Distance from start of section (miles)	(km)	Distance from end of section (miles)	(km)	Distance from Lindisfarne Priory (miles)	(km)	Distance from Heavenfield (miles)	(km)
4	Warkworth	0	0	18.2	29.2	45.8	73.8	50.2	80.8
4	Road at Acklington Park	3.8	6.2	14.3	23.1	49.7	80.0	46.4	74.6
4	Felton	6.7	10.8	11.4	18.4	52.6	84.6	43.5	69.9
4	Weldon Bridge	11.3	18.2	6.9	11.1	57.1	91.9	38.9	62.6
4	Pauperhaugh Bridge	14.9	23.9	3.3	5.3	60.7	97.7	35.3	56.9
4	Rothbury	18.2	29.2	0	0	64.0	103.0	32.0	51.5
5	Rothbury	0	0	14.7	23.7	64.0	103.0	32.0	51.5
5	Lordenshaws car park	2.2	3.5	12.6	20.2	66.2	106.5	29.9	48.0
5	Coquet Cairn	4.6	7.5	10.1	16.2	68.7	110.5	27.4	44.1
5	Harwood village	9.3	15.0	5.4	8.7	73.3	118.0	22.7	36.5
5	Harwood road end	9.8	15.7	5.0	8.0	73.8	118.7	22.3	35.8
5	Knowesgate	13.6	21.9	1.1	1.8	77.6	124.9	18.4	29.7
5	Kirkwhelpington	14.7	23.7	0	0	78.8	126.7	17.3	27.8
6	Kirkwhelpington	0	0	17.3	27.8	78.8	126.7	17.3	27.8
6	Great Bavington	3.2	5.2	14.0	22.6	82.0	131.9	14.0	22.6
6	Little Bavington	4.5	7.2	12.8	20.6	83.2	133.9	12.8	20.6
6	Hallington	6.4	10.3	10.9	17.6	85.1	137.0	10.9	17.6
6	Great Whittington	10.4	16.7	6.9	11.1	89.1	143.4	6.9	11.1
6	B6318 near Halton Shields	12.2	19.6	5.1	8.2	90.9	146.3	5.1	8.2
6	Stagshaw roundabout	14.0	22.5	3.3	5.3	92.7	149.2	3.3	5.3
6	Heavenfield	17.3	27.8	0	0	96.0	154.5	0	0
	Heavenfield to:								
	Wall	1.6	2.5						
	Acomb	2.2	3.5						
	Hexham	4.2	6.8						

Key to Maps

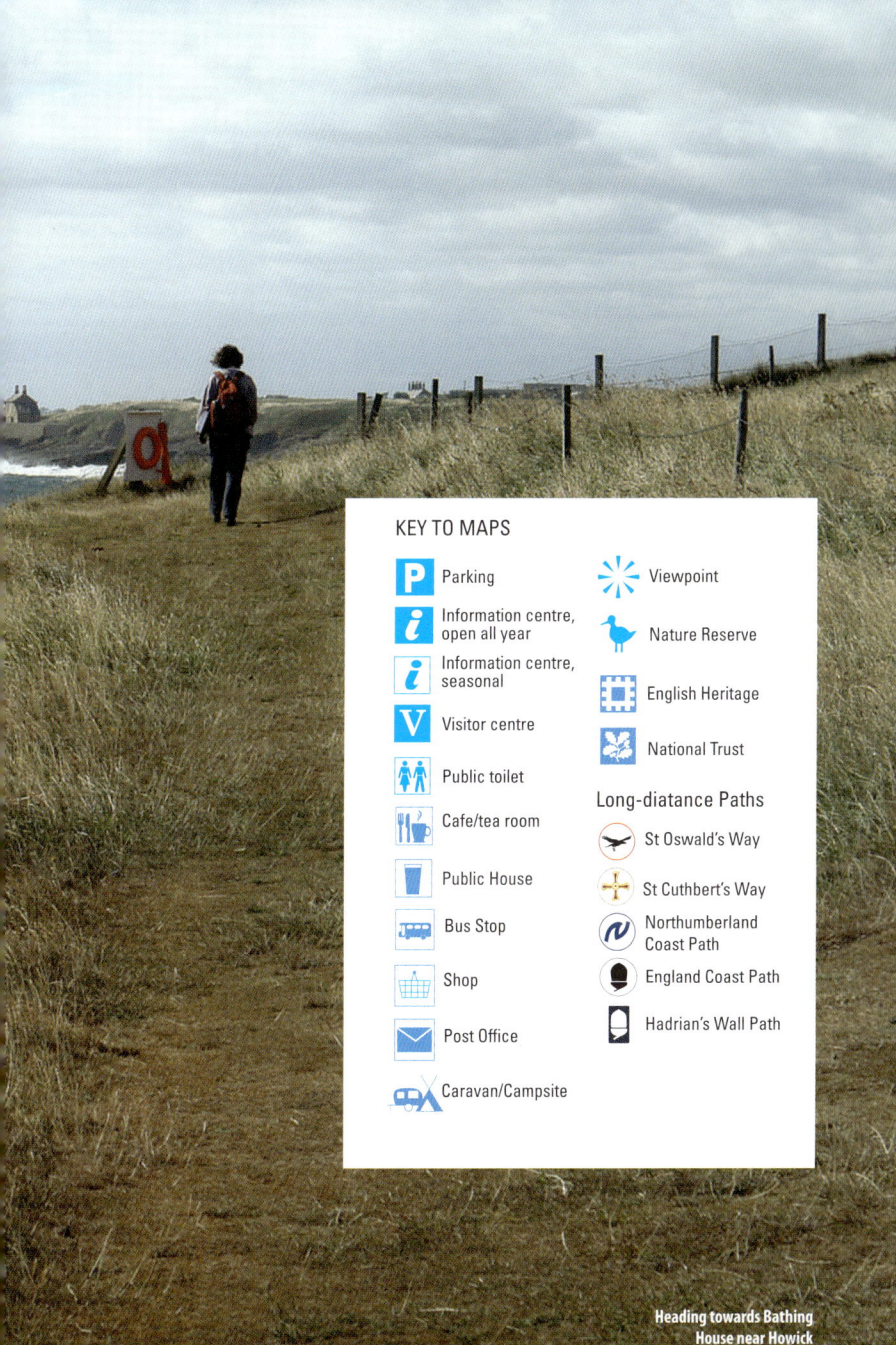

KEY TO MAPS

- **P** Parking
- **i** Information centre, open all year
- **i** Information centre, seasonal
- **V** Visitor centre
- Public toilet
- Cafe/tea room
- Public House
- Bus Stop
- Shop
- Post Office
- Caravan/Campsite
- Viewpoint
- Nature Reserve
- English Heritage
- National Trust

Long-diatance Paths

- St Oswald's Way
- St Cuthbert's Way
- Northumberland Coast Path
- England Coast Path
- Hadrian's Wall Path

Heading towards Bathing House near Howick

Section 1 - Holy Island to Bamburgh
Map A - Holy Island - Belford (Grain Silos)

Holy Island Sands (covered at high tide)
Please check tide times before crossing to/from Holy Island

Lindisfarne National Nature Reserve

SECTION 1 Map A Navigational Points Grid References	
Navigation Point	OS Grid Reference
1	NU 1258 4184
2	NU 1235 4257
3	NU 0794 4270
4	NU 0773 4228
5	NU 0738 4101
6	NU 0699 4012
7	NU 0621 3918
8	NU 0608 3773
9	NU 0674 3588
10	NU 0838 3506
11	NU 0966 3430
12	NU 1087 3389
13	NU 1256 3393

Section 1 - Holy Island to Bamburgh

Holy Island of Lindisfarne

The early history of Lindisfarne is associated with two bishops: St. Aidan and St. Cuthbert. Aidan was bishop until his death in 651 – about sixteen years. Of their monastery on the island, nothing remains other than what is displayed in the excellent Priory Museum. The monastery's most magnificent surviving achievement – the 7th century illuminated manuscript, the Lindisfarne Gospels, is in the British Library in London.

The Anglo-Saxon monastery was attacked by the Vikings in 793 and until 875 when the monks moved to safety on the mainland. The monastery was re-founded as a priory in the late 11th century. The ruins that we see today include the Priory's church of that time and of later 13th century monastic buildings. The Priory is now in the care of English Heritage.

Lindisfarne Castle

Next to the Priory is the parish church of St. Mary the Virgin. Only monks were allowed to worship in the Priory, so a church was needed for the villagers. This building is mainly of the 13th century but several changes have been carried out since then. The church is still the destination for many pilgrims that visit the island.

The other major building on Lindisfarne is the castle. It is built on a dramatic site on a rocky outcrop at the south east of the island. The original fort was constructed by the crown in about 1550 and continued in use until the early 19th century. In 1902, it was bought by Edward Hudson, the founder of the magazine **Country Life**. Hudson commissioned the rising young architect Edwin Lutyens to convert the castle into a summer country home. This is the building we see today and it is now owned by the National Trust.

St Aidan

Lindisfarne Priory

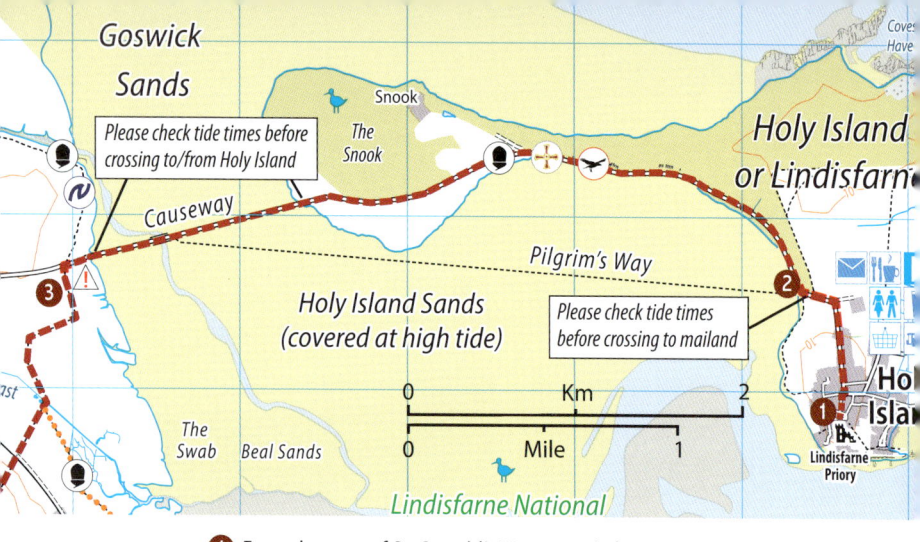

1 From the start of St. Oswald's Way at Lindisfarne Priory, head towards the village, passing to the left of the stone cross. Go straight ahead then, at the road junction, straight on again. Pass the large car park on your right and follow the road down to Holy Island Sands.

Causeway refuge

2 St. Oswald's Way follows the road and causeway across to the mainland. It is also possible to follow the Pilgrims' Way across the Sands, along the line of wooden poles straight ahead. Please note that both these routes are only passable when the tide is out and the Pilgrims' Way, in particular, can be hazardous. You must ensure that you have enough time to complete your crossing before setting off: check tide tables on the **holyislandcrossing-times.northumberland.gov.uk** website, or ask a local Tourist Information Centre for more information.

Pilgrims Way

Holy Island Causeway & Pilgrims' Way

The old route to Lindisfarne, the 2½ -miles long Pilgrims' Way, is across the sands and is marked by long poles that were erected in 1987. Mediaeval pilgrims to the island followed a route marked with stones. Each year, on Good Friday, walkers finishing their Northern Cross Pilgrimage from northern England and southern Scotland carry wooden crosses across the sands on their final leg to the island.

Proposals to join the island permanently to the mainland began in the 1860s and were opposed by the islanders – a permanent railway branch line was also suggested at this time. The present causeway was completed in 1966.

The island remains inaccessible for a few hours either side of high tide. Stranded cars and passengers are still a feature of the causeway and were used to dramatic effect in Roman Polanski's 1966 film *Cul-de-Sac*. Refuge boxes have been provided on both the Pilgrims' Way and the causeway.

Pilgrims' Way refuge. *Photo: Lily Hosking*

Lindisfarne National Nature Reserve

The sands and dunes of Holy Island are part of the Lindisfarne National Nature Reserve. Tidal mudflats, saltmarsh and dunes combine to create a place that is home to fascinating plants and to a food supply that attracts bird visitors from thousands of miles away. The reserve protects a long stretch of coast, as far south as Budle Bay.

Huge flocks of birds spend time on the reserve and six internationally important species of wildfowl and wading birds spend the winter here, including the light-bellied brent goose from Svalbard in Arctic Norway. About half of the world population of this species come to feed on the mud flats each year, and this is their only regular wintering site in Britain.

Lindisfarne also has international recognition: it is a 'Ramsar site', a wetland of international significance, amongst other environmental designations.

Lindisfarne Nature Reserve

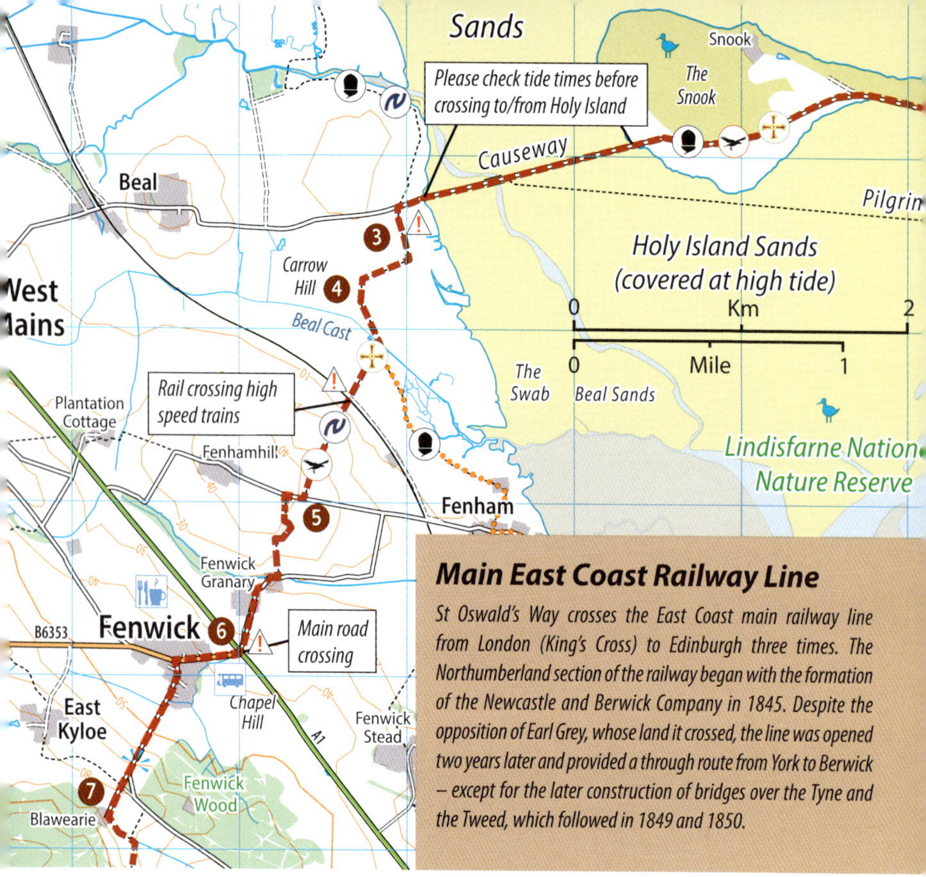

Main East Coast Railway Line

St Oswald's Way crosses the East Coast main railway line from London (King's Cross) to Edinburgh three times. The Northumberland section of the railway began with the formation of the Newcastle and Berwick Company in 1845. Despite the opposition of Earl Grey, whose land it crossed, the line was opened two years later and provided a through route from York to Berwick – except for the later construction of bridges over the Tyne and the Tweed, which followed in 1849 and 1850.

❸ After reaching the mainland, turn left along the path past the concrete cubes. From this point St. Oswald's Way (and St. Cuthbert's Way and the England Coast Path) joins the Northumberland Coast Path: follow the distinctive waymarking and signposts for the Northumberland Coast Path, featuring the symbol for the North Sea Trail. After 300 yards, the route turns right through a gate into a field. Follow the path ahead up the right-hand side of the field to reach a track.

Coastal Defences

The large concrete cubes are anti-tank blocks. During World War 2, the wide beaches of Northumberland were seen as a prime potential German invasion area, either as a diversion from a larger landing in the south, or to target the rich coal fields of the North East. As a result, much of the county's coastline was heavily defended with pillboxes (small buildings for soldiers with rifles or machine guns), gun emplacements and anti-tank blocks. A lot of these heavy concrete remains can still be seen in various coastal sections of the walk, with the blocks near the causeway being

④ Turn left along the track to reach a field. Bear left across to the far corner of the field. Cross the bridge over the stream and follow the path ahead, (leaving the England Coast Path) up the right-hand side of the field to a railway line. Take great care when crossing the East Coast main railway as high-speed trains frequently pass this point. Use the telephone provided to check that it is safe to cross. Follow the field-edge path uphill to meet a lane.

⑤ Turn right then, about 100 yards later, turn left along the first track. Follow the winding track through to another lane. Turn right and continue past Fenwick Granary to reach the A1 main road.

⑥ Cross the A1 with care and go straight ahead into the village of Fenwick. At the first road junction, turn left and follow this road up the hill to another junction. Go straight ahead on the more minor road, rather than bearing left.

⑦ Just before the house on the right (Blawearie), turn left and follow the path along the field edges. With Kyloe Woods on your right hand side, continue along the path. The route joins the course of an old lane known as Dolly Gibson's Lonnen and enters Shiellow Woods.

The Great North Road

The "premier highway in Britain" originated in roman roads and ancient tracks. However, as a through route it could be said to date from 1603 when King James I (of England) instituted a postal service from London to Berwick. The modern A1 runs roughly parallel to it, but bypasses the towns that were originally linked. The Northumberland part of the Great North Road probably began as tracks linking the main towns of Newcastle, Morpeth, Alnwick and Berwick. St. Oswald's Way crosses the old route three times at Fenwick (where it is also the present A1), Belford and Felton.

Fenwick

Fenwick

Fenwick today is a village with a small number of houses: its shops and school have disappeared. It was originally part of the Haggerston Estate and the houses were occupied by estate workers. The present day village hall was originally a granary. It later became a reading room where the men of the village could play billiards and read the papers. Access to the upper floor is by external stone steps.

From Dolly Gibson's Lonnen

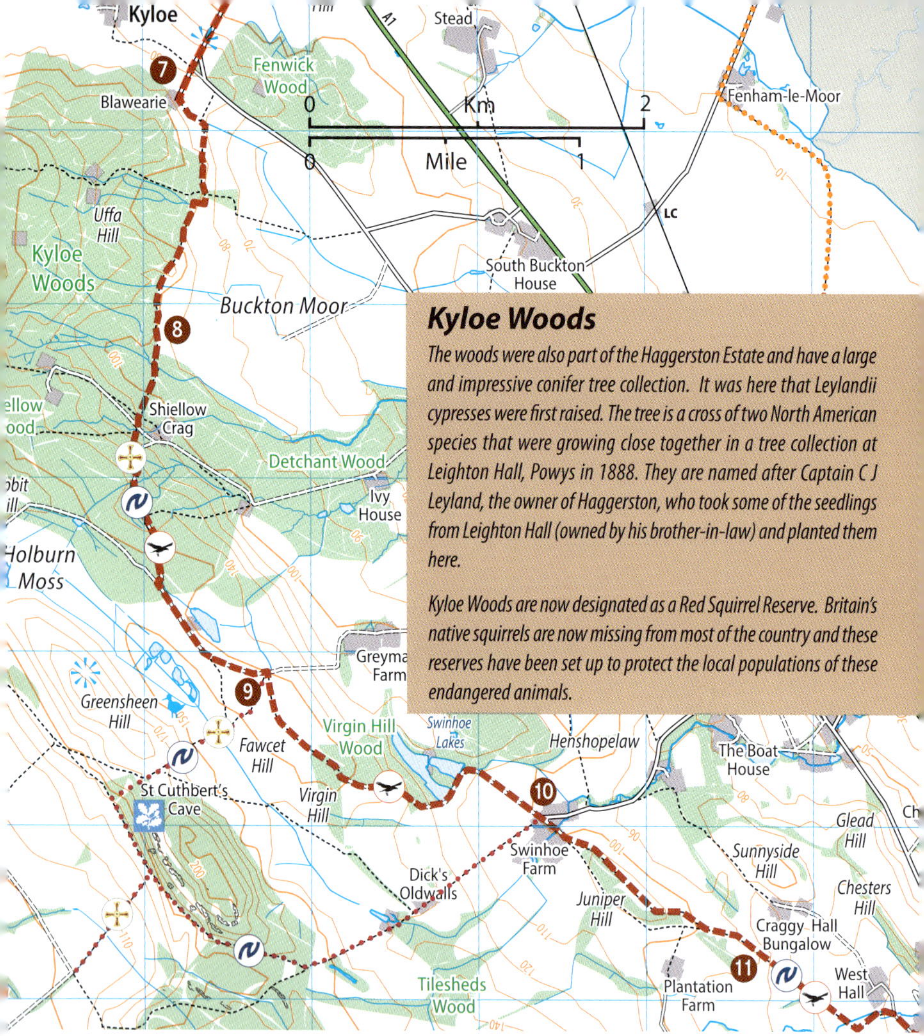

Kyloe Woods

The woods were also part of the Haggerston Estate and have a large and impressive conifer tree collection. It was here that Leylandii cypresses were first raised. The tree is a cross of two North American species that were growing close together in a tree collection at Leighton Hall, Powys in 1888. They are named after Captain C J Leyland, the owner of Haggerston, who took some of the seedlings from Leighton Hall (owned by his brother-in-law) and planted them here.

Kyloe Woods are now designated as a Red Squirrel Reserve. Britain's native squirrels are now missing from most of the country and these reserves have been set up to protect the local populations of these endangered animals.

Near Greensheen Hill

8 Go straight ahead on the waymarked footpath through the trees. Cross a forestry track and follow the footpath to join another track. Follow the track straight ahead to a T-junction. Turn left on a public bridleway and follow the track out of the woods. Continue along the track with Greensheen Hill over to your right. To the left are lovely views of the coast, including Holy Island and Lindisfarne Castle, the Farne Islands and Bamburgh Castle.

9 At a gate on the right, turn right into a field. Here, St. Oswald's Way continues with the Northumberland Coast Path, while St. Cuthbert's Way heads off to the right on a bridleway to St. Cuthbert's Cave (which is about ½ mile away and makes an interesting side trip). Follow the path along the left-hand side of the field, keeping the crags to your left, and into more forestry. Follow the main track, past Swinhoe Lakes and on to Swinhoe Farm.

St Cuthbert's Cave
Photo: Tony Derbyshire

10 At the farm, cross the lane and walk between the buildings, through a gateway and to a small gate at the top of the track into a field. Walk up the field and around the crag to a mast. Go through the gate at the mast and turn right. Follow the path around the tops of the fields, with Sunnyside Crags over to your left and, eventually, woodland on your right. At the end of the wood, go through the gate and bear left. Follow the path across the field and down to reach a track.

St. Cuthbert's Cave

When the monks of Lindisfarne fled from Viking attacks in 875, they took the sacred remains of St. Cuthbert with them. Legend has it that this scenic natural sandstone overhang was one of the places that they stopped. Other stories suggest that, when alive, Cuthbert used the cave as a hermitage. The site is now managed by the National Trust

11 Go straight ahead along field-edge paths then a track, eventually passing Westhall on your left. Turn left off the track, walk alongside a fence and then along the right-hand side of a stream to reach a lane. Turn right and follow the lane to a road. Turn left and head into the centre of the village of Belford, near to the church.

Belford area

Just before Belford lies Westhall farmhouse, a square, castellated building, built in the gothic style in 1837. It is the site of a fortified tower house, which was surrounded by a moat. Nothing of the house now exists, but remains of part of the moat can still be seen across the field.

Belford developed as a post town in which, before the coming of the railway, the Blue Bell was a thriving coaching inn. The inn remains at the centre of the town close to the St. Mary's Church. Although the church retains a Norman chancel arch, the building today largely dates from the rebuilding, by the well-known Newcastle architect John Dobson, in 1829. In the corner of the churchyard, there is a watch house. These were built to shelter guards who had to keep watch for grave robbers, who came to steal the bodies of the dead for use in medical schools in the mid 19th century.

Belford's market cross was probably built around 1741 and it retains much of its character and former importance as a market town. The A1 passed through the centre, along the old Great North Road, until the 1980s.

The 18th century mansion house, Belford Hall, is set in parkland to the north-east of the church. The Belford Estate owned most of the town, including its gas and water supplies, until it was sold off in 1923.

Spindlestone Ducket

It is more likely to have been a dovecot. It dates from the 18th century and has a slate roof with a ball on top. The Ducket was built on the site of a medieval moated farmstead.

Belford market place

⑫ (Please note that the route may be changed at this point, moving to the north-east of Belford and rejoining the England Coast Path at Cragmill. Check the St Oswald's Way website and follow any signs. Continue from point 13.) Turn right along High Street (the former A1). About ¼ mile later, just after the entrance to the golf club, turn left on a path that runs alongside the Belford Burn. After crossing a track, follow the path to meet the present A1. Cross the road with care and go straight ahead on the footpath, past a large number of grain silos to reach the East Coast mainline railway. After using the telephone provided, carefully cross the railway. Follow the path ahead with a ditch on your right to meet the England Coast Path again.

⑬ Turn right through a gate and go over a disused railway. Cross the field to reach a track. Go straight ahead then, at the next bend, go straight on across the field to a gate then to a stile. Cross the stile and walk with the wall, then the remains of a hedge, on your right. Ahead to the right, the small round tower of Spindlestone Ducket can be seen.

Spindlestone Ducket

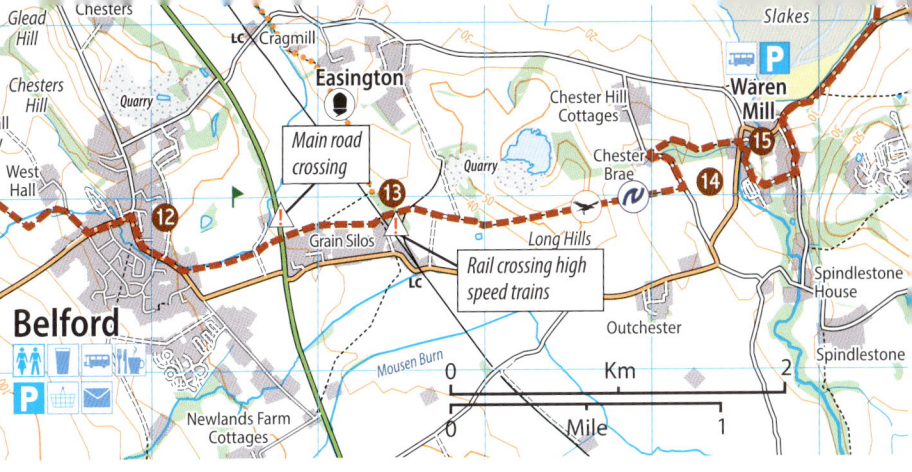

Waren Mill

14 After reaching a lane, turn left. Walk down the lane, then turn right on a footpath opposite a small building. Follow the path, with the woodland on your right, to reach the road at Waren Mill.

15 Turn right, then turn left on a driveway to a campsite. Just before the campsite gate, turn left onto a footpath parallel to the driveway. Follow the fenced path beside the campsite, then go straight on up a track to meet a lane. Turn left and follow the lane down to a road on the edge of Budle Bay. At the road, turn right. Cross to the footpath on the outside of the bend when safe to do so, and follow the road next to the bay.

16 When the road starts to bend to the right towards the top of the hill, take the path through to a gate on the left. Follow the path along the left-hand side of the fields. At the end of the last field, go through the gate at the edge of the bay and turn right. Shortly afterwards, turn left past an old lime kiln. Walk along the left-hand side of the next field, with views across the bay back to Lindisfarne Castle, and continue along the path to Heather Cottages.

Looking over the old pier at Budle Bay

Section 1 - Holy Island to Bamburgh
Map B - Belford (Grain Silos) - Bamburgh

Bamburgh Lighthouse and Stag Rocks

For over 80 years, the small lighthouse at Blackrocks Point near Bamburgh has given a guide to shipping in passage along the coast as well as to vessels in the waters around the Farne Islands. The lighthouse is unmanned and was originally built in 1910 as a circular, metal-framed tower with acetylene gas lamps. It was modernised in the 1970s and the new electric lamp was put on top of the acetylene fuel store building. It is the most northerly land-based lighthouse in England.

Nearby are Harkess Rocks, known locally as Stag Rocks. There is a white stag painted on one of the rocks but nobody is sure why. One suggestion is that it was because a stag jumped into the sea to escape hunters. Another theory is that it was painted by Italian prisoners of war during World War 2.

Stag Rock & Bamburgh Lighthouse.

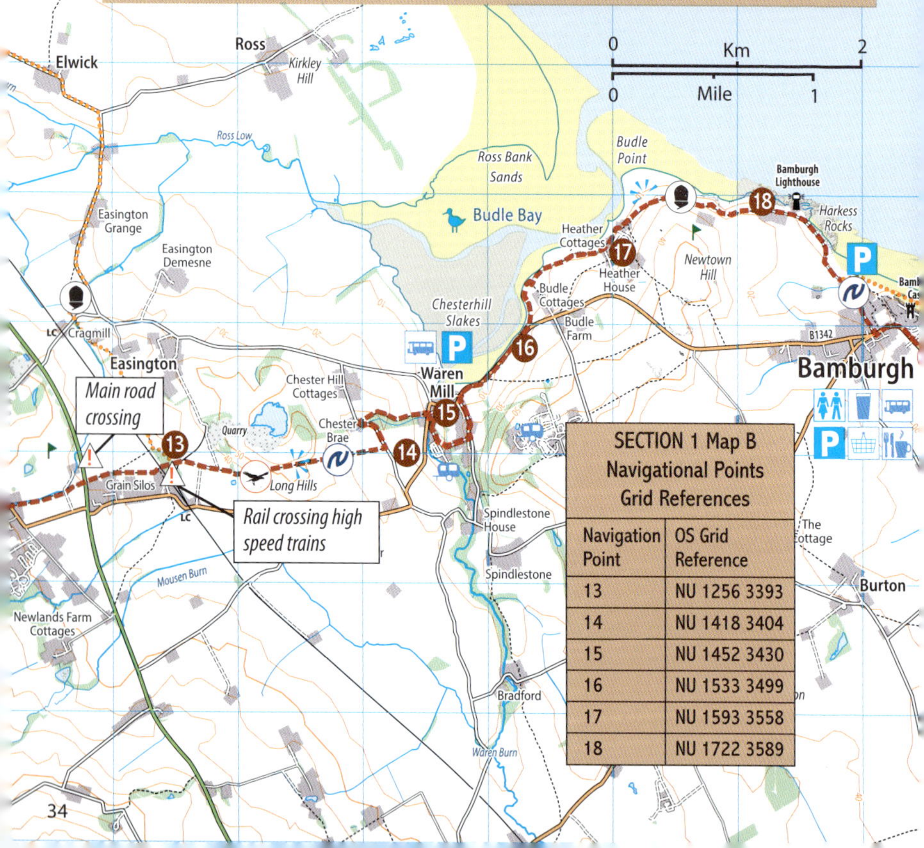

SECTION 1 Map B Navigational Points Grid References	
Navigation Point	OS Grid Reference
13	NU 1256 3393
14	NU 1418 3404
15	NU 1452 3430
16	NU 1533 3499
17	NU 1593 3558
18	NU 1722 3589

⑰ When reaching the buildings, turn left along the path. Just before the beach, bear right on a path through the dunes. Pass to the right of the remains of an old concrete building then a World War 2 gun emplacement. Go straight on and follow the path through the dunes and overlooking the bay. As the Farne Islands and Bamburgh Castle come into view, follow the path to the left of the golf course.

⑱ At the golf clubhouse, follow the road towards Bamburgh. On reaching the houses, leave the England Coast Path and continue along the road into the centre of the village.

Gun emplacement Budle Bay

Bamburgh from the north

Section 2 - Bamburgh to Craster

Bamburgh

The imposing structure of Bamburgh Castle dominates this part of the Northumberland coast. Bamburgh was the site of King Oswald's royal headquarters but archaeology, including by the Bamburgh Research Project, has revealed a complex and long occupation of the site, probably dating back to an Iron Age hill fort.

The Anglo-Saxon Chronicle records that Bamburgh was founded by King Ida. He was (probably) Oswald's great grandfather and founder of the Bernician dynasty. The castle may well be the site of a church that, according to Bede, contained the relics of Oswald at one time.

Bamburgh was an important royal stronghold until 1464 when, during the War of the Roses, it became the first English castle to be destroyed by gunfire. It was to remain a ruin until it was bought by Lord Crewe, in the 18th century. In the 1890s, the castle was sold to the armament manufacturer Lord Armstrong who undertook the extensive re-building to convert it to his version of the archetypal castle, which it remains to this day.

Amongst many other interesting features within the castle, there is a small archaeological museum that contains a number of interesting finds. From Oswald's era, these include fragments of a highly decorated stone chair (perhaps the king's throne) and the remains of an extraordinarily sophisticated sword that could only have belonged to a king. A vast Anglo-Saxon cemetery of Oswald's time has been discovered to the south of the Castle that, it is thought, may contain as many as 1,200 bodies.

Although the castle dominates the village, the rest of Bamburgh also has a fascinating history. In the 13th century it was home to a Dominican friary and also a leper colony!

Top: **Bamburgh Village overlooked by the castle.**

Centre: **Bamburgh Castle.**

Bottom: **St Aidan's Church and the Grace Darling Memorial.**

The first church in Bamburgh was a wooden one built in 635 by Aidan and Oswald, probably on the site of today's church. The impressive St. Aidan's Church was mainly constructed by a group of Augustinian canons between 1170 and 1230. The church was heavily restored in the 19th century and contains a St. Oswald's Chapel.

At the church there is also a monument to Grace Darling. Grace was born in Bamburgh in 1815, but spent much of her life living on the Farne Islands with her father, who was a lighthouse keeper. The Grace Darling Museum, across the road from the church, illustrates her life on Longstone, the story of the famous rescue and the lighthouse, amongst a variety of other facilities.

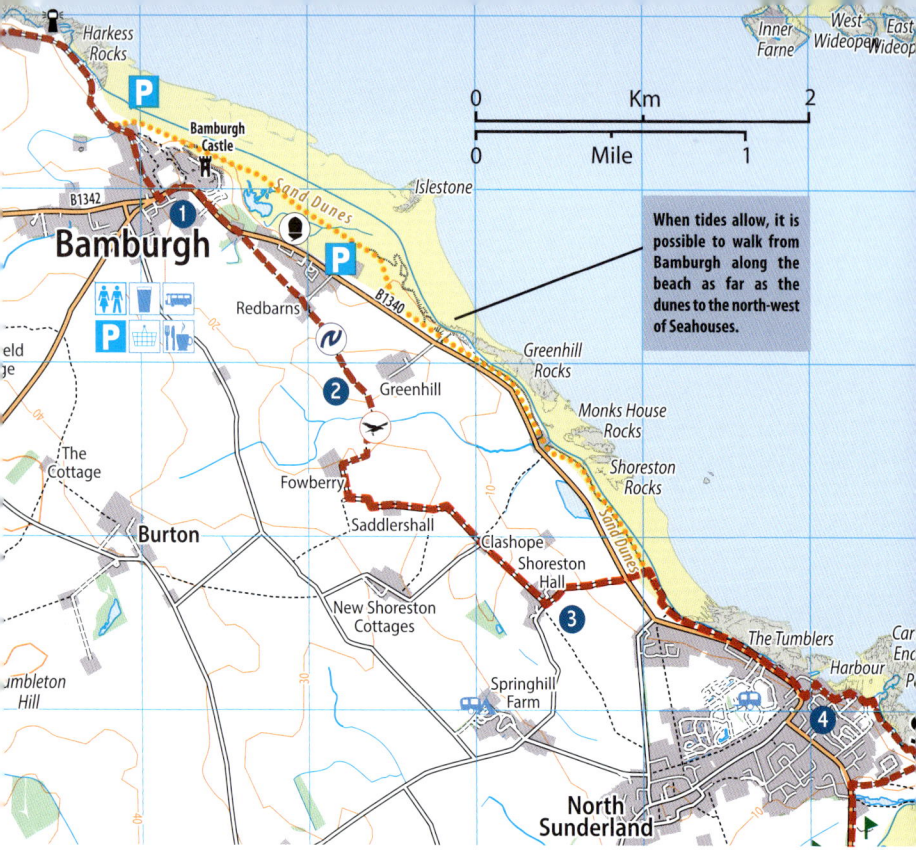

1 Leave Bamburgh on the main road out of the village, passing the castle on your left. About 250 yards after the main village car park, leave the road and bear right on a footpath across the field towards the right-hand buildings of those ahead (Redbarns, the site of the former Bamburgh Gas Works). Pass just to the left of the buildings and follow the path ahead through the fields, keeping to the right of the hedge. The Cheviot Hills are often visible in the distance to your right and the Farne Islands are out at sea to your left.

2 After passing Greenhill Farm to your left, walk with a wall on your left then over to a gate. Go through the gate and walk with a fence, then a hedge on your right. Turn right onto a track to reach Fowberry. Turn left along the lane and follow it through to a T-junction. Turn left, passing Shoreston Hall and continue until you reach the main coastal road.

3 Cross the main road and walk into the dunes. After about 100 yards and just before the beach, turn right, rejoining the England Coast Path. Follow the path through the dunes until you reach a footpath along the top of some low cliffs near to the road. Looking backwards, on a clear day you can see Lindisfarne Castle and Bamburgh Castle, as well as boats going to and from Seahouses and the Farne Islands. Follow the footpath into the village of Seahouses.

Farne Islands

There are twenty-eight of the Farne Islands, although some are covered at high tide. The nearest of the larger islands, with a lighthouse, is Inner Farne. This was the home, and favourite place, of St Cuthbert. He lived there from late in the 670s until 685 when he was persuaded to become Bishop of Lindisfarne.

Inner Farne with Longstone Lighthouse and Outer Farne in the distance

Further out, on the island of Longstone, is another lighthouse. This was built in 1826 and its first keeper was William Darling, the father of Grace. She became famous in 1838 after the paddle steamer, the SS Forfarshire, struck a rock and was wrecked, half a mile from Longstone lighthouse, where William was stationed. The two of them rowed out through the raging sea to rescue nine survivors who were clinging onto the rock. News of the event soon spread across the country and Grace became the first woman to be awarded the RNLI Medal for Gallantry. Unfortunately, she died of tuberculosis just four years later.

Puffins
John Hallowell

The Farnes are the home to thousands of breeding seabirds from late May until the end of July. These include arctic terns, sandwich terns, shags, kittiwakes, guillemots and puffins. Mention should also be made of St Cuthbert's own favourite eider ducks: known as Cuddy (or St Cuthbert) Ducks. There is also a large population of grey seals. The islands are now managed by the National Trust and visits can be made by boat trip from Seahouses.

Seahouses harbour, gateway to the Farne Islands.

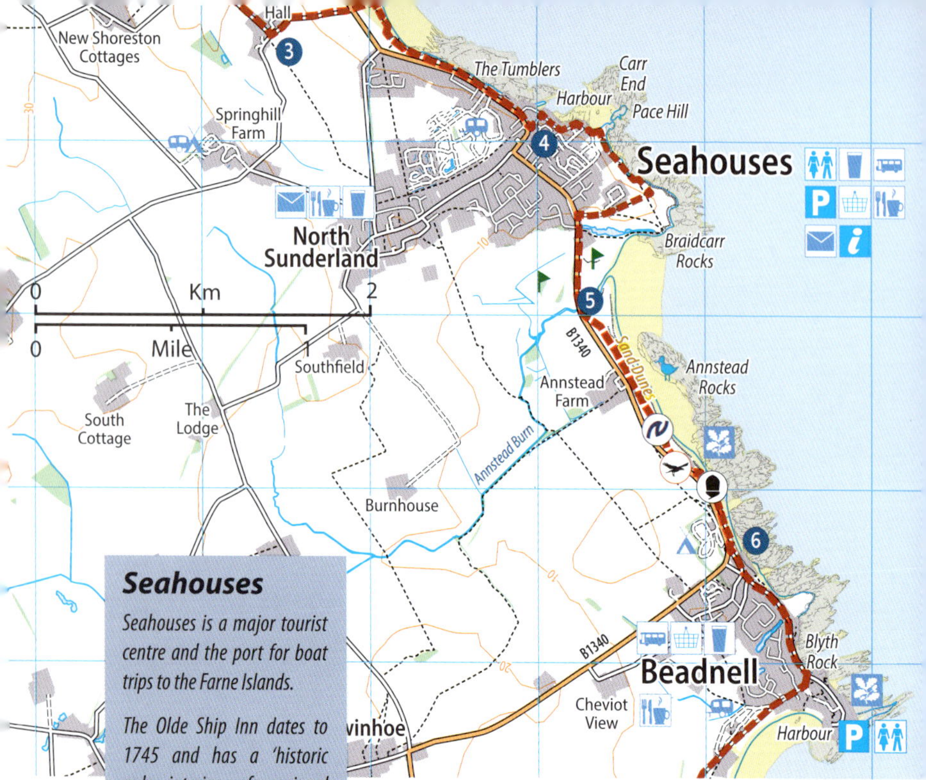

Seahouses

Seahouses is a major tourist centre and the port for boat trips to the Farne Islands.

The Olde Ship Inn dates to 1745 and has a 'historic pub interior of regional importance'. The public bar was originally two rooms but has altered little in the last 70 years.

Two rocky promontories have made Seahouses a natural harbour for at least seven hundred years. The development of the fishing trade in the 17th century, and lime burning in the early 18th century, led to the development of the harbour facilities. The limekilns that can be seen at the harbour continued in use until 1858.

On the rocks to the east of the harbour is a small stone building (the Powder House) that was built in 1886 to store gunpowder used to create the Long Pier and New Harbour.

4 At the roundabout, turn left along the road and down to the harbour. Follow the road around to the right of the harbour, then walk on a footpath along the coast. The path then enters a golf course (be aware of flying golf balls as you follow the waymark posts). Go straight ahead for 50 yards then turn right along a path through the course to reach a gateway. Follow the driveway ahead to a road. Turn left, walk along the roadside path and pass the golf course.

5 Just after the bridge over the Annstead Burn, bear left onto a path through Annstead Dunes. Bear right to go through a gate and follow the path, roughly parallel to the road. After rejoining the road, walk past Links House then bear left onto another path along the dunes. Eventually reach a road junction at the edge of the village of Beadnell.

Bloody Cranesbill, Northumberland's county flower.

Annstead Dunes

Annstead Dunes is a nature reserve managed by Northumberland Wildlife Trust and consists of a strip of mature sand dunes. The Trust has fenced areas of the dunes to enable grazing with Exmoor ponies and this has helped to open up the grass to allow more of the dune plants to thrive. Selective removal of the scrub, such as sycamore, is also undertaken to preserve the dune conditions. Plants to look out for include bloody cranesbill (Northumberland's county flower), lady's bedstraw, bird's-foot-trefoil and restharrow.

6 Turn left and follow the road towards the village. Opposite the first junction, there is a road (The Haven) that takes you to the centre of Beadnell. The route, however, takes the road to the left for half a mile. At the junction, it is possible to bear left for an interesting visit to Beadnell Harbour and, perhaps, an alternative route along the beach of Beadnell Bay. St. Oswald's Way, however, follows the road around to the right and past the car park.

Beadnell

The attractive village of Beadnell includes the interesting parish church of St. Ebba, who was the sister of St. Oswald. One of the village pubs, the Craster Arms, contains the remains of a medieval tower house

On the rocks to the north-east of Beadnell Harbour (known as Ebb's Nook) are the remains of the medieval chapel of St. Ebba. It was excavated in 1853 and the remains suggested that it had been built not long after Aidan's arrival at Lindisfarne. Little is known of the chapel although the name suggests a link with Oswald's sister.

The impressive group of three large, and disused, limekilns that stand near the harbour were built in 1798 and are now in the care of the National Trust. Limekilns were used to produce lime by burning limestone with coal. The lime was widely used to improve the quality of agricultural land.

The harbour is of a similar date to the kilns and has the distinction of being the only west-facing harbour on the east coast of England.

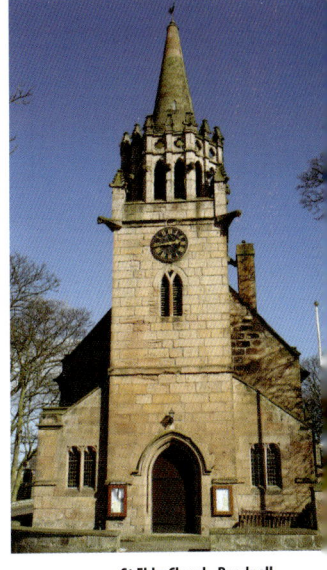

St Ebbs Church, Beadnell

Beadnell Harbour and the lime kilns

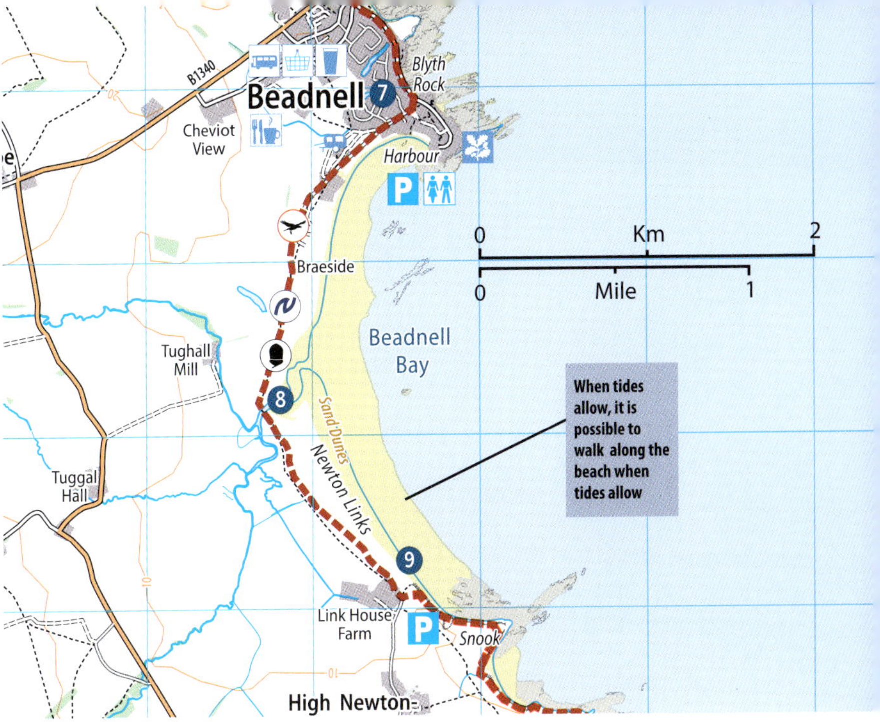

7 Take the left-hand option of the two driveways and walk with the caravan park on your right and the dunes on your left. Then enter a second caravan park and follow the driveway. After 200 yards, take the right-hand fork and follow this through to rough land on the edge of the dunes. Follow the path ahead past Tughall Dunes and through to a footbridge over the Long Nanny Burn.

8 Continue straight on along the main path through Newton Links. After passing Newton Links House and through a gate, you arrive at a car park.

Bridge over Long Nanny burn

Newton Links

Newton Links is one of the best examples of sand dunes with species-rich vegetation on the Northumberland Coast, and has been designated as a Site of Special Scientific Interest (SSSI). The site also includes saltmarsh around the Long Nanny inlet and the dunes provide a breeding site for a colony of little terns, arctic terns and ringed plovers.

Newton Links

The Snook

9 Go into the car park, then go through a gate on your left. Bear right across the dunes then turn right and walk with a fence on your left, along the top of the dunes. Follow the path parallel to the beach, then cut across the end of Snook Point. Walk along the path close to the shore and then around Newton Point, with views of Dunstanburgh Castle in the distance. Follow the coastal path to the small village of Low Newton-by-the-Sea and turn left at the road.

10 It is possible to walk along the beach at Embleton Bay as an alternative route, when tides allow. Otherwise, turn right just before The Square at the bottom of the village. Follow the access road around the back of the cottages and pub. Go straight ahead on a track parallel to the coast. Pass to the left of a cottage on a footpath into Newton Pool Nature Reserve. Follow the paths around to the right and up to the top of a slope, overlooking the Pool.

Low Newton by-the-Sea

The Square at Low Newton with buildings around three sides and the sea along the fourth are 18th century fisherman's cottages. It is one of only two surviving such squares in England. The only two-storey building in the square is the pub, The Ship Inn. The cottages were improved in the middle of the 19th century. This was necessary, apparently, as a contemporary writer described them as "not pretty nor pleasing". This is not a description that applies today as they are excellently preserved.

The building on the hilltop to the north of the Square is Watch House, a former coastguard station. It was built in the early 19th century and provides a splendid view down the coast to Dunstanburgh Castle.

Road to Low Newton by-the-Sea with Dunstanburgh Castle on the horizon

Low Newton by-the-Sea

11 Turn left and follow the path to the left of the golf course and past the beach huts, with wonderful views across Embleton Bay. The path then drops down a bank and runs through rough ground to the left of the golf course. After reaching a stream and bridge on your left, turn right onto the path across the course.

On the path above Newton Pool

Newton Pool Nature Reserve

Just to the south of Low Newton is Newton Pool Nature Reserve, owned by the National Trust. The reserve is set behind the dunes and is a freshwater pool ringed with rushes and with a number of islands. There are hides from which migrant waders and wildfowl can often be seen, especially in winter.

Overlooking Embleton Bay and Coquet Island on the horizon

⑫ Just before reaching the club house car park, turn left and follow the path around and along the edge of the golf course.

⑬ Pass the parking area near Dunstan Steads and follow the main path to the right of the golf course. Finally cross the course and head towards the dramatic cliffs of Rumble Churn and Castle Point. Pass to the right of Dunstanburgh Castle and up the sloping path to the left to reach the entrance gate to the castle. Turn right and head towards the sea, turning right when you reach the shore. After reaching a gate, continue on the path to the village of Craster.

Rumble Churn

Dunstanburgh Castle standing on the Great Whin Sill

The Great Whin Sill

The cliffs at Dunstanburgh are some of the many dramatic features of the Great Whin Sill. It is composed of the hard rock known as dolerite and was formed by molten rock forced through layers of earlier rock by the movement of the earth's tectonic plates. The name derives from terms used by northern English quarrymen. "Sill" was used to describe a more or less horizontal body of rock and "whin" was used to describe dark and hard rocks.

Outcrops of the Whin Sill can be seen at various places on St. Oswald's Way, and they are associated with many of the most famous places in Northumberland. The castles of Lindisfarne, Bamburgh and Dunstanburgh are all built on the Whin Sill, as is much of Hadrian's Wall. Out at sea, the Farne Islands are also formed by the Whin Sill.

'Whin' is also the local name for gorse, which can be seen growing on the whinstone in many places.

Dunstanburgh Castle

The second Earl of Lancaster, grandson of King Henry III, had the original castle built in 1313-6 (on the site of an Anglo-Saxon fortified town). Lancaster was the leading – and richest - noble in England and had stormy relations with the then king, Edward II (as he did with nearly everybody else). Dunstanburgh was conceived as a safe retreat and he wanted, and got, an immense and lavishly equipped castle. He was never to use it for its purpose: when he led a rebellion against the king in 1322, he was captured at Boroughbridge in Yorkshire and subsequently beheaded before he could retreat to Dunstanburgh.

In the early 15th century, the castle fell into some disrepair and it wasn't until the late 1430s that major repairs were carried out. Later that century, during the Wars of the Roses, Dunstanburgh was successfully attacked three times and much damage was done.

The remains that are seen today date mainly from the earliest period. The huge scale of the castle can be appreciated from the surviving walls enclosing eleven acres and the grandeur from what is left of the gatehouse. This gatehouse, with the inner ward behind, was the main domestic quarters of the castle. Further along the south wall is the Constable's Tower, which was the residence of the Castle's commanding officer, and, at the end of the wall, Egyncleugh Tower. The other remaining tower, Lilburn Tower, is in the west wall and was probably a watchtower.

To the south of the castle is the site of the castle's harbour. In 1314, a ditch was dug from here around the western side of the castle towards Embleton Bay in an attempt to make the promontory into an island. The ditch can still be seen in places.

Section 3 - Craster to Warkworth

Craster

The word 'Craster' is derived from 'Craucestr' meaning an old fort inhabited by crows. The village owes its name to the family that has lived in nearby Craster Tower – which originated as a fortified pele tower – since the early 15th century. Originally, the village clustered around the tower and only developed around the harbour in around 1700. It was the Craster family who built the current harbour in 1906 in memory of Captain John Craster, who was killed in active service in India in 1904.

The harbour only took its present shape in the late 1930s when the silos that had stood above the (remaining) arch at the end of the south pier were removed. These silos had been constructed in 1914 to assist in the shipping of whinstone. The silos were 27 metres long and were filled by huge buckets that travelled by cable over the tops of the houses. The quarry at Craster provided stone that was used for kerbs in London and Roker Pier in Sunderland. The quarry is now partly a car park and also the Northumberland Wildlife Trust's Arnold Memorial Reserve.

However, Craster's real fame comes from its smokehouses. In the 19th century, the North Sea was teeming with herring, and some 20 boats supplied four kipper / herring yards in the village. Great barrels of salt herring were exported to Germany and Russia, and fresh kippers (smoked herring) were dispatched to Billingsgate Market in London. In the season, crews of herring-girls each split and gutted 2,000 fish a day. Today, only the first smokehouse, dating from 1856, remains operating – Robson's still make Craster Kippers even though the herring no longer comes from the North Sea.

Craster was just a small part of the British herring industry, which also involved other ports from Northern Scotland to East Anglia. The exploitation was utterly unsustainable and catastrophic for herring stocks: the enterprise had mostly collapsed by early in the 20th century.

Craster offers dramatic views of Dunstanburgh Castle to the north – a view that was painted by JMW Turner.

From top to bottom: **Craster**

Craster harbour

Kipper shed

Dunstanburgh from south of Craster

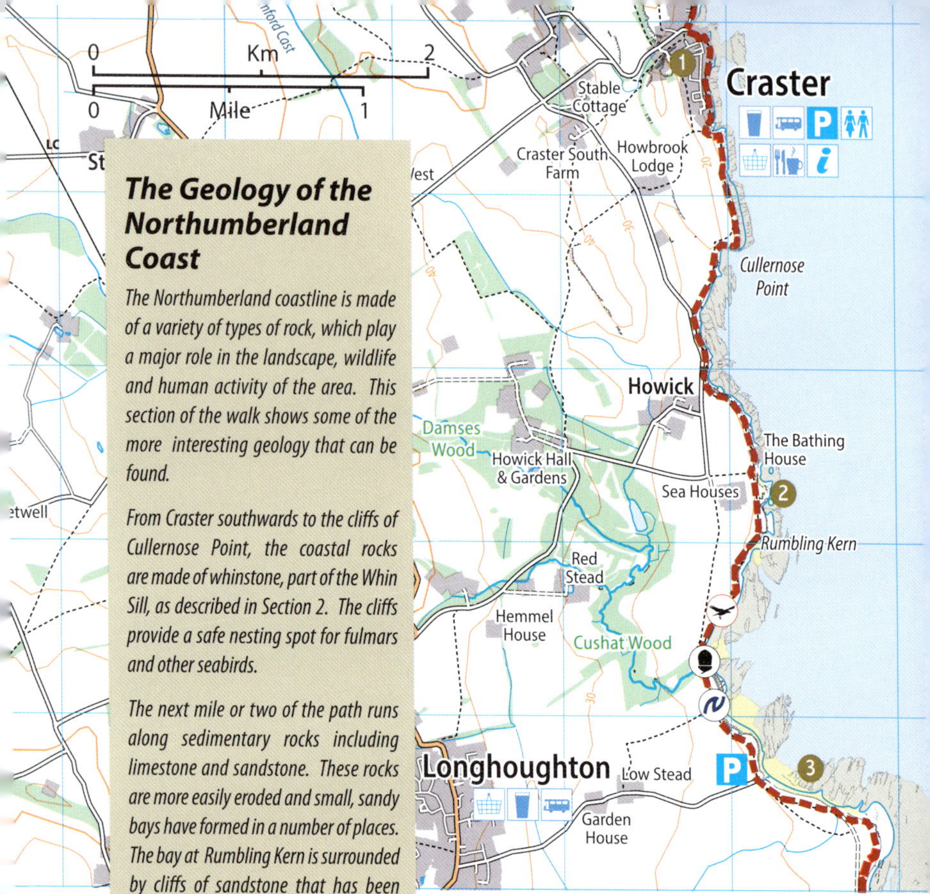

The Geology of the Northumberland Coast

The Northumberland coastline is made of a variety of types of rock, which play a major role in the landscape, wildlife and human activity of the area. This section of the walk shows some of the more interesting geology that can be found.

From Craster southwards to the cliffs of Cullernose Point, the coastal rocks are made of whinstone, part of the Whin Sill, as described in Section 2. The cliffs provide a safe nesting spot for fulmars and other seabirds.

The next mile or two of the path runs along sedimentary rocks including limestone and sandstone. These rocks are more easily eroded and small, sandy bays have formed in a number of places. The bay at Rumbling Kern is surrounded by cliffs of sandstone that has been quarried in the past.

Either side of Boulmer, the rock changes again to a type of coarse-grained sandstone, known here as the Longhoughton Grit. The outcrops of this rock extend out to sea, forming reefs or 'steels'. A geological fault at Boulmer has resulted in a gap in the reef and allowed the development of a safe harbour.

1 From the centre of Craster, walk along the road to the right of the harbour. Turn left just before the Jolly Fisherman pub, then right through the gate and past the back of the building. Follow the path past the village and along the coast. Pass the spectacular cliffs of Cullernose Point and continue along the coastal path to The Bathing House.

Cullernose Point

The Bathing House

The Bathing House is a (private) 18th century cottage remodelled in the 1840s for the Grey family. Steps led from the cottage to a quarried out rock pool.

A short distance inland is Howick Hall, home of the Grey family since 1319. The family includes the 2nd Earl Grey, Britain's Prime Minister from 1830-4, who was responsible for the Great Reform Act of 1832. He was also the 'father' of Earl Grey tea. While Prime Minister, Earl Grey sent a diplomatic mission to China and, by chance, his envoy saved the life of a Chinese mandarin. In gratitude, the mandarin

The Bathing House

sent the earl a delightfully scented tea, along with its recipe. The special ingredient with which it was flavoured was oil of bergamot. The earl's drawing room soon became famous for its tea and, in due course, the family gave permission for the blend to be sold in public. Today, Earl Grey tea is the world's most popular blended tea and is found in more than 90 countries.

The gardens at Howick Hall are regularly open to the public.

2 After passing the building, bear left on the path southwards along the coast. Three-quarters of a mile further on, you pass the site of Howick's Stone Age settlement to your right and then a footbridge over Howick Burn. Follow the track ahead and along past the small parking area at Low Stead Links.

Reconstruction of Stone Age hut at Howick

Howick Stone Age Settlement

Excavations by archaeologists in 2000 to 2002 at Howick Haven revealed the remains of a mesolithic hut dating from just after 8,000 BC, possibly the oldest house yet found in Britain. The people living in this Stone Age hut were "hunter-gatherers" since they would have obtained their food by hunting, gathering and fishing. At that time the sea was about four and a half metres below today's level and a few hundred metres further out. The hut was 6 metres in diameter and similar to a tepee. A smaller reconstruction used to stand on top of the cliff at Howick.

Bridge over Howick Burn

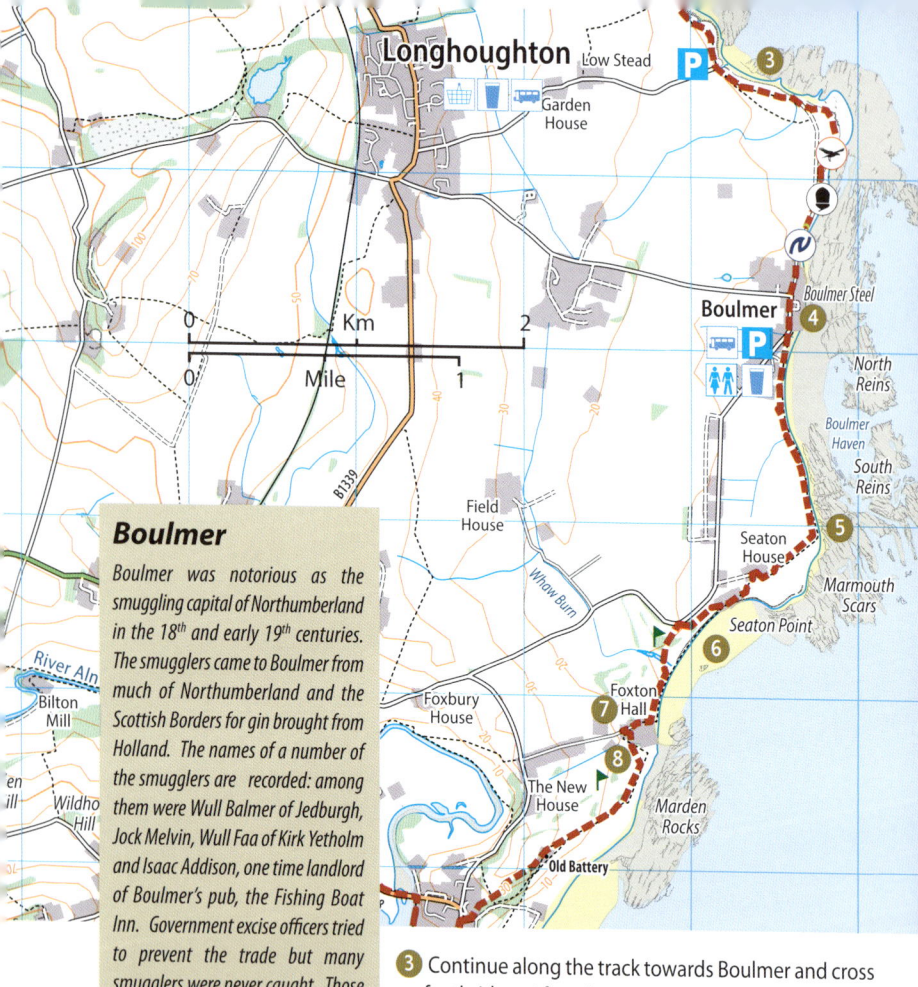

Boulmer

Boulmer was notorious as the smuggling capital of Northumberland in the 18th and early 19th centuries. The smugglers came to Boulmer from much of Northumberland and the Scottish Borders for gin brought from Holland. The names of a number of the smugglers are recorded: among them were Wull Balmer of Jedburgh, Jock Melvin, Wull Faa of Kirk Yetholm and Isaac Addison, one time landlord of Boulmer's pub, the Fishing Boat Inn. Government excise officers tried to prevent the trade but many smugglers were never caught. Those who were often escaped conviction because few people would testify against the gangs, either through fear of retribution or because they benefitted from the smuggling.

Today, Boulmer is better known for its RAF station. RAF Boulmer began in 1940 as a decoy airfield to attract enemy planes away from the real airfield at Acklington, a few miles to the south. It is now a key station of the RAF's Battlespace Management Force, providing surveillance of UK airspace and tactical control of combat and support aircraft.

❸ Continue along the track towards Boulmer and cross a footbridge. After about 50 yards, leave the track and bear left on a path around the grassy headland. Rejoin the track and follow it, then the road, into the village of Boulmer.

Boulmer

④ Go straight ahead at the junction in the village then, after the right-hand bend, turn left onto a footpath that runs along the coast. It is possible to walk on the beach from here towards Seaton Point. Otherwise, walk through the car parking area, then along the coastal path and through to a gate. Follow the path ahead past the large navigation posts and on to reach a caravan park.

⑤ Turn right on a grassy track past the caravans and towards Seaton House. Follow the track past Seaton House then turn left on a track opposite the last building. Bear right on a footpath and walk alongside a fence and to the left of the wooden huts to reach a track that goes down to the beach.

⑥ Cross the track and walk up the bank opposite. Pass through a gate then cross the field to another gate. After a few yards, turn right and walk along the right-hand side of a golf course then turn left to cross the fairway. Follow the path through the course, past a pond, then keep to the left of the course and near to the beach. When you reach a track, turn right and follow it uphill.

⑦ Pass to the right of the golf clubhouse, then around the back of the building. Follow the path back to the left of the golf course, then along the coast and eventually back onto the course.

Approaching Alnmouth from the north

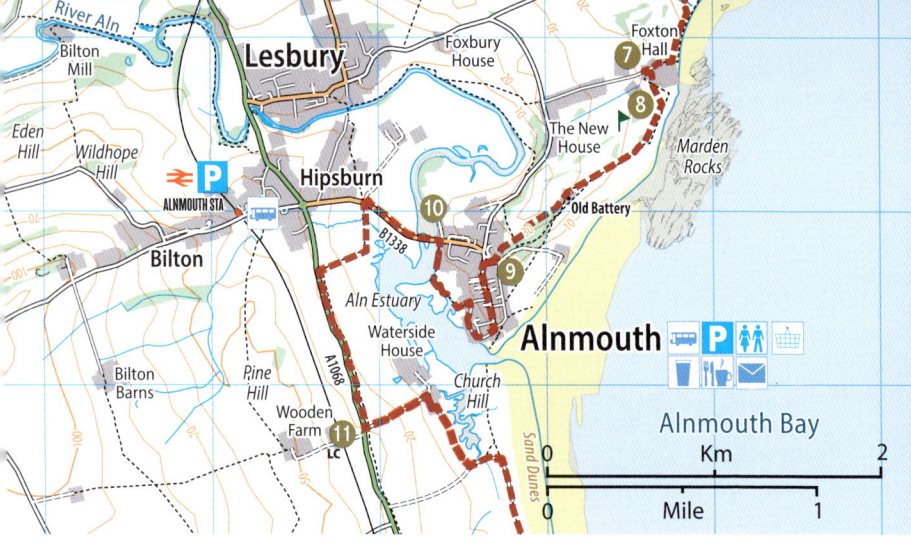

⑧ Walk alongside the fence through the course and be aware of flying golf balls. Follow the path ahead through the rough ground. At the Old Battery on the left, go straight on. Pass the beacon, then go straight ahead and follow the path down to a road

⑨ Turn right, then left at the next junction. Walk along the main street through Alnmouth. At the bottom, turn right onto Riverside Road and follow it by the side of the Aln Estuary. Just after a recreation area, turn left on a footpath known as "Lovers Walk". Follow the path around to meet the road at The Duchess' Bridge.

The Old Battery

Above the beach at Alnmouth is The Old Battery, built in 1861 (because of a war scare) by the Duke of Northumberland for the use of the 2nd Northumberland (Percy) Artillery Volunteer Corps. Their practice sessions included shooting at a floating target near the mouth of the river. Two of the early guns from the battery are preserved at Alnwick Castle. During World War 2, the battery was modified to create a pillbox, and some concrete blocks guard the nearby path down to the beach.

❿ Cross the road then turn left over the footbridge alongside the road bridge. Walk along the road for a short way, then follow the path to the right of the hedge. About 400 yards later, turn left at a gate, cross the road and go straight ahead onto a track between fields (part of the Coast and Castles Cycle Route). Follow the cycle track between the fields then parallel to the road.

Alnmouth

Alnmouth, or St. Waleric as it was originally called, was founded as a medieval borough in the 12th century. It was to develop as a grain port and shipbuilding centre until 1336, when the village was virtually destroyed by the Scots. Twelve years later the Black Death wiped out one third of the population.

In the 17th and 18th centuries, the port thrived again by exporting grain from the Tyne valley, and at one time there were 16 granaries in the village. The grain (often oats) was brought along the Hexham to Alnmouth "Corn Road", a turnpike built in the 1750s that also meets St. Oswald's Way at Rothbury and Little Bavington. Hindmarsh Hall, the village's community centre, is a converted granary.

Smuggling was also a large part of Alnmouth life and it was described as "a small seaport town famous for its wickedness" by John Wesley, the founder of the Methodist Church.

In those days, a narrow ridge of land linked Alnmouth with Church Hill, which can be seen across the mouth of the river. The hill was much larger then, and fragments of an Anglo-Saxon cross have been found there. The River Aln entered the sea to the south of Church Hill until 1806, when a violent storm breached the ridge and changed the course of the river. This made the harbour much less attractive for shipping, as the new channel was less deep than the old one.

The growth of tourism in Victorian times helped Alnmouth to recover, leading to the building of expensive villas and the picturesque, peaceful village of today.

Church Hill, Alnmouth

Alnmouth houses

Duchess's Bridge, Alnmouth

Section 3 - Craster to Warkworth
Map B - Alnmouth - Warkworth

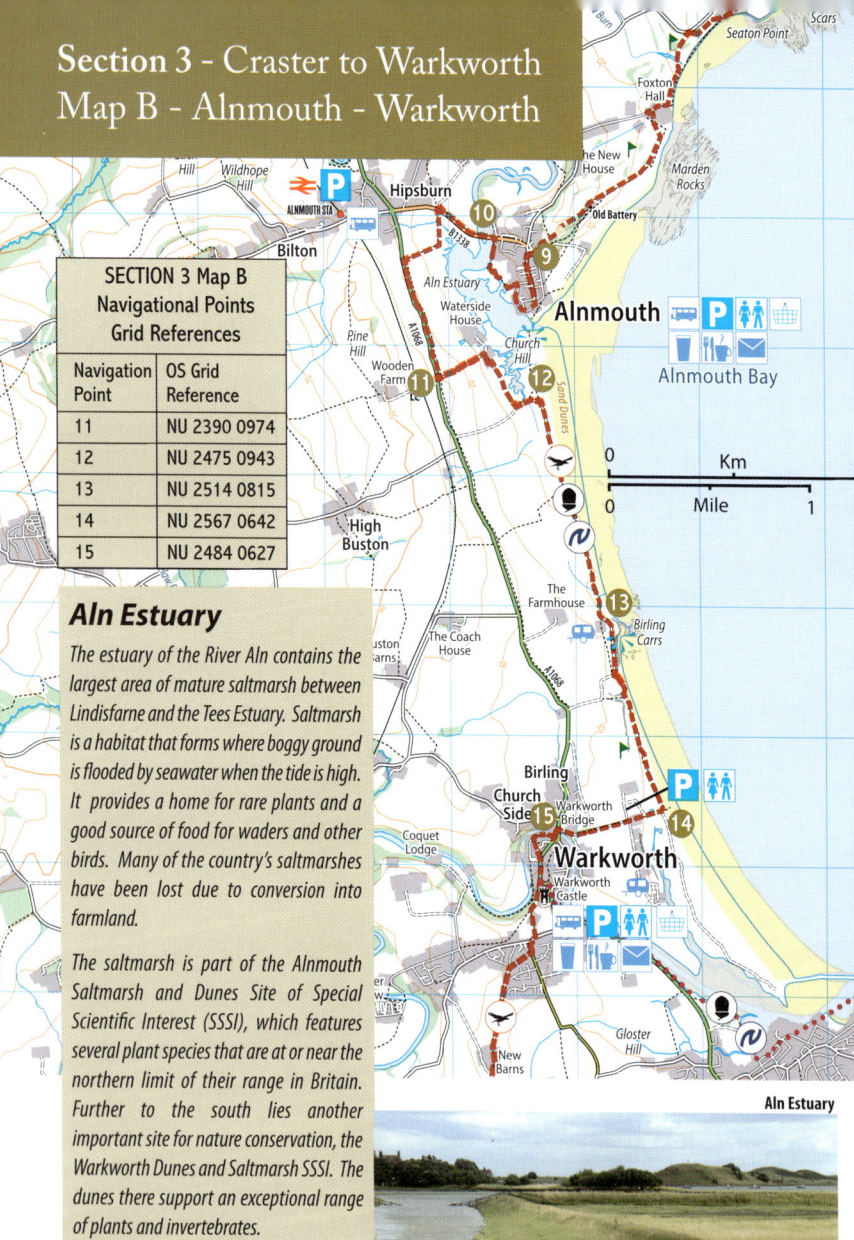

SECTION 3 Map B Navigational Points Grid References	
Navigation Point	OS Grid Reference
11	NU 2390 0974
12	NU 2475 0943
13	NU 2514 0815
14	NU 2567 0642
15	NU 2484 0627

Aln Estuary

The estuary of the River Aln contains the largest area of mature saltmarsh between Lindisfarne and the Tees Estuary. Saltmarsh is a habitat that forms where boggy ground is flooded by seawater when the tide is high. It provides a home for rare plants and a good source of food for waders and other birds. Many of the country's saltmarshes have been lost due to conversion into farmland.

The saltmarsh is part of the Alnmouth Saltmarsh and Dunes Site of Special Scientific Interest (SSSI), which features several plant species that are at or near the northern limit of their range in Britain. Further to the south lies another important site for nature conservation, the Warkworth Dunes and Saltmarsh SSSI. The dunes there support an exceptional range of plants and invertebrates.

The building near to the track at the southern end of the Aln Estuary is said to be an old guano storage shed. Alnmouth used to import guano (bird droppings used as fertiliser), and this spot would have been far enough away from the village to keep the dreadful smell at bay.

Aln Estuary

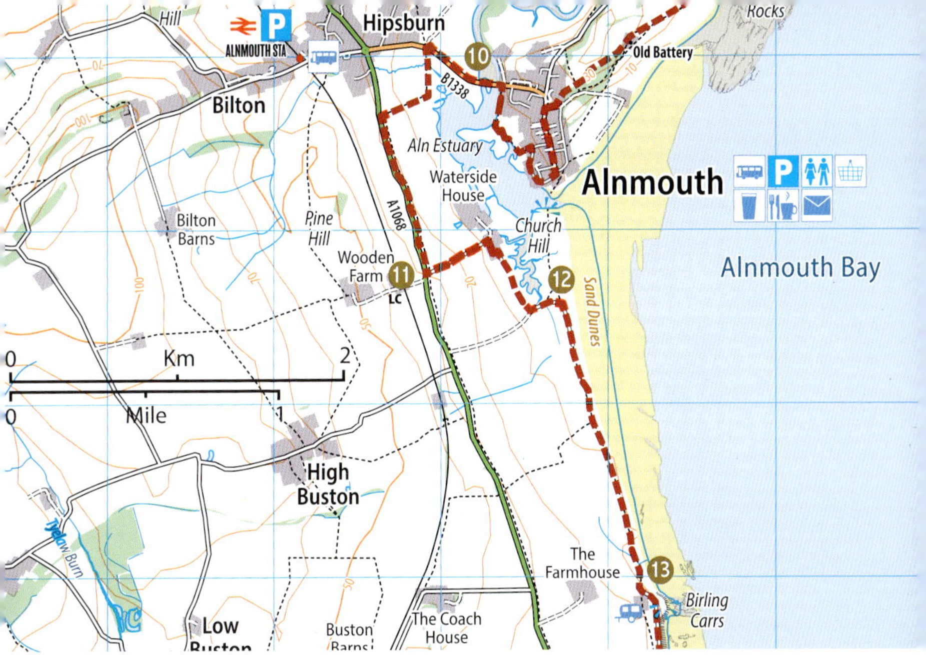

11 At the first junction, turn left and head along the lane down towards the estuary. Just before the buildings at the bottom, turn right onto a track. Follow the track around the buildings and with a fence on your right. Go through a small gate and follow the path to the right of the hedge. When reaching a rough track, turn left and follow it around to the right, with the dunes on your left and the remains of the old guano shed on the right.

Alnmouth from the south

12 As an alternative, when the tide allows, you can make your way through the dunes to the beach, then along towards Warkworth Dunes. St. Oswald's Way continues along the track, through a gateway, then straight ahead on the path parallel to the coastline. Follow the path up onto and along the dunes.

Guano shed, Alnmouth estuary

57

13 After crossing a footbridge, bear right on a track through a caravan park then along the edge of a golf course, with lovely views ahead to Coquet Island and Amble. Turn left onto a path just before the track crosses the course. Follow the path parallel to the beach. Continue on the path, with the dunes on your left and the golf course on your right, to reach a track.

14 Turn right and follow the track straight ahead up to Warkworth Dunes Picnic site. Carry straight on along a path to the left of the hedge and parallel to the road, then down the road to a junction on the edge of Warkworth.

15 Leaving the England Coast Path behind, cross the road carefully and cross the River Coquet on the old bridge. Go through the gatehouse then turn sharp right onto a riverside path. Follow this path (Monks Walk) until you reach a parking area. Turn left past St. Lawrence's Church and into the centre of the village.

Cycle path near Alnmouth

Coast and Castles Cycle Route

This popular cycling trail runs from Newcastle to Edinburgh, a distance of 200 miles, including much of the Northumberland coast. It is also part of an even longer route, the National Cycle Network Route 1, which runs all the way from Dover to John O' Groats.

Coquet Island

Coquet Island is about a mile off the coast and it and its white square lighthouse are clearly visible from the path. The lighthouse was built in 1841 and its first lighthouse keeper was Grace Darling's brother.

The island has many religious connections and was famous for its monastery in Anglo-Saxon times. Later, there was a hermitage on the island: Henry, the hermit of Coquet Island, is buried at Tynemouth.

Today, the island is managed by the Royal Society for the Protection of Birds. It has a large number of puffins and is particularly famous for the only colony of roseate terns in Britain. Landing is not allowed on the island but boat trips around it are available in late spring and summer from Amble.

Warkworth Bridge and Gatehouse

The older bridge over the Coquet at Warkworth was built in the last quarter of the 14th century. It has two arches and a gatehouse at the south end. The road into the village used to run through the archway at the gatehouse, which guarded the entrance to the bridge. Warkworth Bridge is one of only two fortified medieval bridges in Britain; the other is in Monmouth.

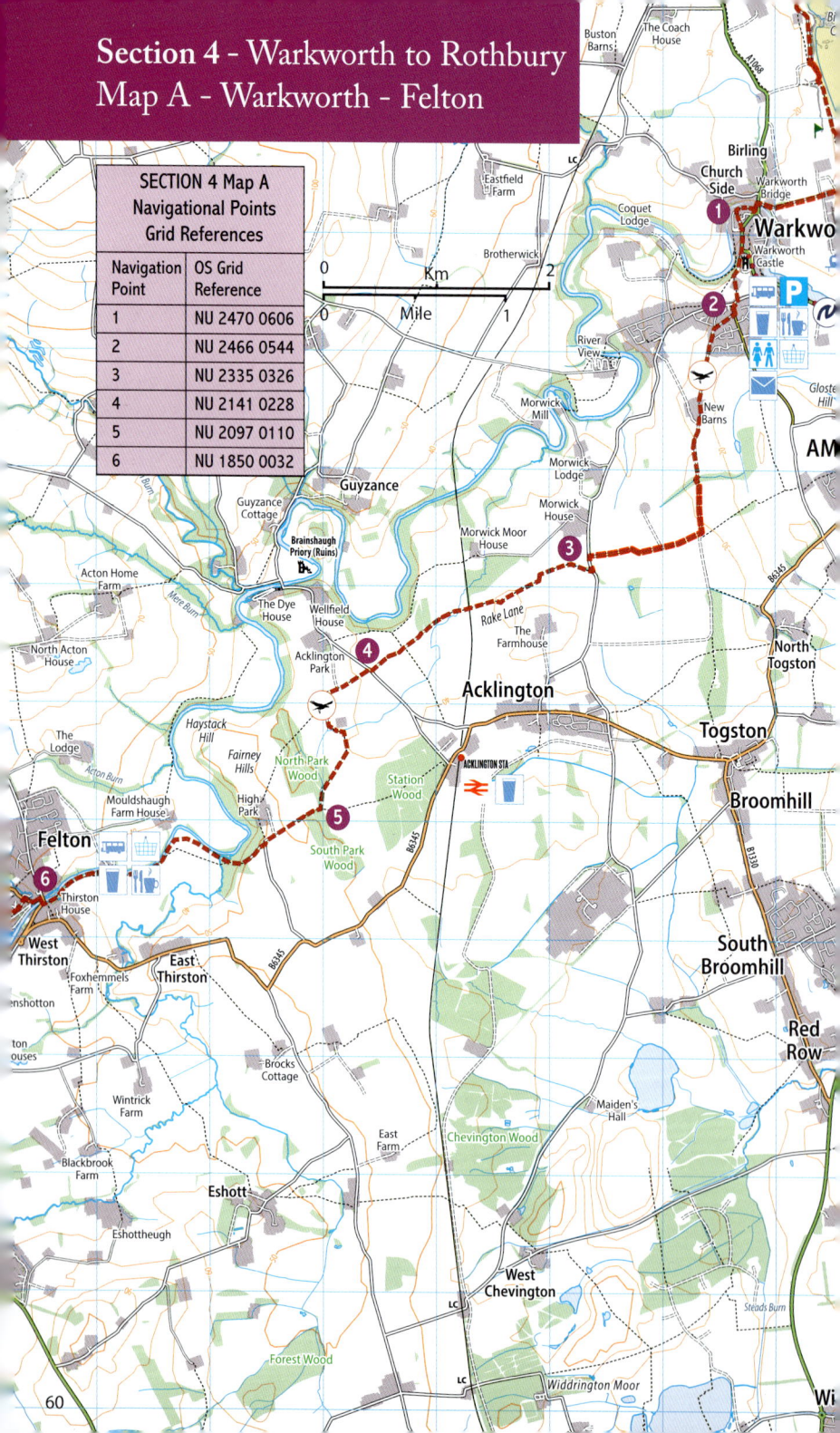

Section 4 - Warkworth to Rothbury

Warkworth

The old village of Warkworth is enclosed in a loop of the River Coquet and is thought to be of Anglo-Saxon origin. There was a wooden Saxon church here founded in the 730s by King Ceolwulf, who gave it to the abbot and monks of Holy Island. The present early 12th century church of St Lawrence stands on its site. Much of this Norman church remains today, although there have been later additions. In a Scottish raid in 1174, Warkworth was set on fire and 300 people, who had taken refuge in the church, were put to death.

Warkworth flourished in the mediaeval period when it was a harbour and market town. It still retains an essentially mediaeval layout, with its defended bridge and gatehouse at one end, leading up to the castle at the highest point of the village. The village also has a number of fine buildings of the eighteenth and nineteenth centuries and most of Castle Street is of this date.

The village, however, is dominated by the castle: "this worm-eaten hold of ragged stone" according to Shakespeare's induction to Henry IV Part 2. Nevertheless, the castle was substantially finished by Shakespeare's time.

The earliest castle was an 11th century 'motte and bailey'. In 1158, Henry II gave Warkworth to Roger FitzRichard who began the building of the first stone castle and of this period the gatehouse survives. Ownership eventually passed to Henry de Percy IV, who became the first Earl of Northumberland, and had the keep built in the 1380s and 90s. This building is today the most substantial remains at the castle.

The ownership of the Warkworth Castle passed back and forth between the Percy family and the royal family for centuries. Eventually, the cost of maintaining the castle was so great that the Percys gave it to the nation in 1922. It is now cared for by English Heritage.

Reached by boat from the south of the Coquet is the unusual fourteenth century structure of Warkworth Hermitage. The chapel and the adjoining sanctuary were carved out of the sandstone rock in about 1330-40. They are fairly small (the chapel itself is just over six metres by 2 metres) and a great deal of skill must have been needed to carve out the architectural detail. In the 15th century, small domestic buildings were added to the face of the rock.

Top: **St. Lawrence Church**
Centre: **Warkworth Castle.**
Bottom: **Warkworth Market Cross**

According to tradition, the first hermit and builder of the Hermitage was Sir Bertram, a knight who mistakenly killed his lover, Lady Isabel Widdrington, and his brother as he tried to rescue her from the Scots, causing him to renounce the world.

River Coquet and Coquet Valley Woodlands SSSI

The River Coquet flows for about 57 miles (90km) across Northumberland, from the Cheviot Hills to the sea below Warkworth. It is a relatively natural fast-flowing upland river with characteristic wildlife. The Coquet is one of the most important angling rivers in the north of England, with large runs of sea trout and salmon.

The lower and middle reaches of the river provide undisturbed habitat for otters, and the rich insect life also provides food for a wide variety of bat colonies that roost and rear their young within the valley, particularly around Brinkburn Priory.

River Coquet near Warkworth

The Coquet valley has several woodlands that are long-established and relatively unmodified by planting. There are few such woodlands now left in Northumberland and most are confined to steep river valleys, as along the Coquet below Rothbury. Red squirrels can still be found in these woods.

These excellent wildlife habitats have led to the river, and much of the land adjacent to it, being designated as a Site of Special Scientific Interest (SSSI).

New Barns and Morwick

To the south of New Barns is an area that was part of the large Chester House opencast coal workings. The area was restored to farmland, with tracks and hedges, in 1999. The funnel-like structure on the hill nearby is a concrete water tower that was constructed in 1970.

① From the centre of Warkworth, head up the street towards the castle. Instead of turning left with the road at the top, go straight ahead on a footpath that runs to the right of the castle. Ignore the path that goes down to the river and go straight on, passing the castle. Follow the surfaced path past the clubhouse and ground of Warkworth Cricket Club to reach a road.

② Turn right, then left onto Guilden Road, and right again along Warkworth Avenue. At the end of the road, bear left on a track. Carry straight on past the farm buildings at New Barns. Follow the track ahead then between the fields. At a junction (2/3 mile after New Barns), turn right and follow the rough track, keeping straight on, with the water tower on your right, until reaching a road.

③ Cross the road when safe and turn left. Walk along the side of the road for 100 yards, then turn right along a bridleway (Rake Lane). Follow the winding, grassy old lane and, when reaching the bridge, go straight ahead under the railway. Continue along the lane until reaching a road.

Water tower near Morwick

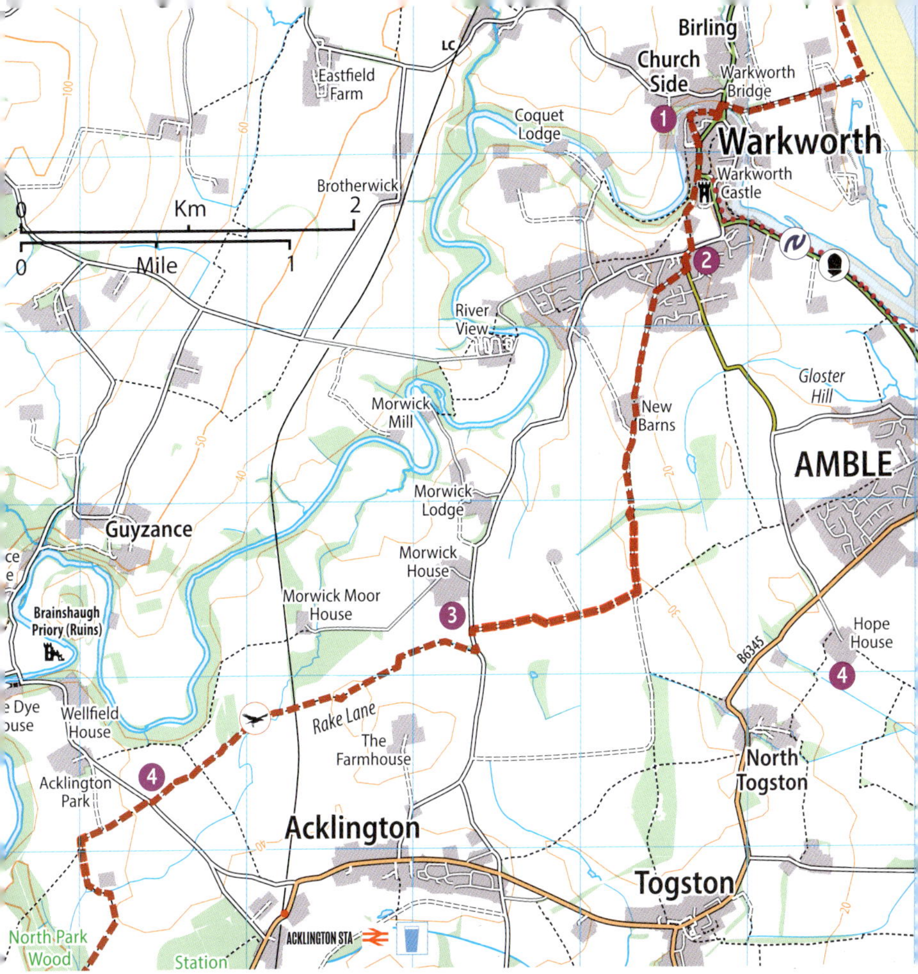

④ Go straight ahead on the bridleway opposite, until reaching a stone track. Carry straight on and follow the track, passing a small, overgrown pond on your left, and then into a field. Turn right and follow the path, with the field boundaries on your right. Join a track and go straight ahead to the corner of the field.

Rake Lane

5 Turn right through the gateway and follow the track to its end. Briefly join a tarmac lane that swings to the left, then turn right onto a public footpath. Follow the track down to the Coquet and walk along the riverside through to the road at West Thirston. Cross the road then cross the River Coquet into Felton using the old bridge.

Old Bridge, Felton

Felton

The village of Felton lay on the old Great North Road and the village developed as a staging post with inns, shops and services. The Old Bridge across the Coquet was probably built in the 15th century. The bridge is built of sandstone and each pier has pointed cutwaters to help the water flow past them. Historical records show that there has been a bridge of some kind here since at least the 12th century, and there is also evidence of an early ford across the river. The bridge was an important part of the old road but now carries only pedestrians.

A key date in Felton's history was 1216. The Northern barons, unwilling to pay taxes to the English King John, had met at Felton Park in the previous year and decided to do homage to the Scottish King Alexander: John had the village burnt down. Some 500 years later, Felton Park was to be a base for the Jacobite rebellion of 1715. The village took a different view in 1745 and welcomed the Duke of Cumberland who passed through on his way to fight at Culloden against the Jacobites. He is said to have referred to Felton as a "loyal little village".

6 Turn left after the bridge, then follow the road to the right at the war memorial. At the next junction, turn left towards the Church of St. Michael and All Saints. At the church that, contrary to first impressions, really does have a roof, bear left on a track then through a gate into a field. Follow the track, then bear slightly left on the footpath across the field. Over to the right can be seen the church at Felton Park.

St Michael and All Angels parish Church

Felton Churches

Felton's large and interesting parish Church of St. Michael and All Angels has a high 19th century roof over its chancel and very low roofs elsewhere. Much of the rest of the church dates from the 13th and 14th centuries with the belfry having been rebuilt some 300 years later.

The churchyard is managed by volunteer parishioners to encourage wildlife. The area is divided into four sections, managed to provide four different types of habitat. Wild flowers have been sown and a variety of bird and other boxes have been provided. You are welcome to visit the churchyard and the church is also open on most days.

The Church of St. Mary, which you can see to the right of the path, was built in the Gothic style in 1857 for Thomas Riddell, who lived next door at Felton Park. The church used to be connected to the house by a corridor. The church served the Roman Catholic parish until 2005 but is now closed.

Near, Felton

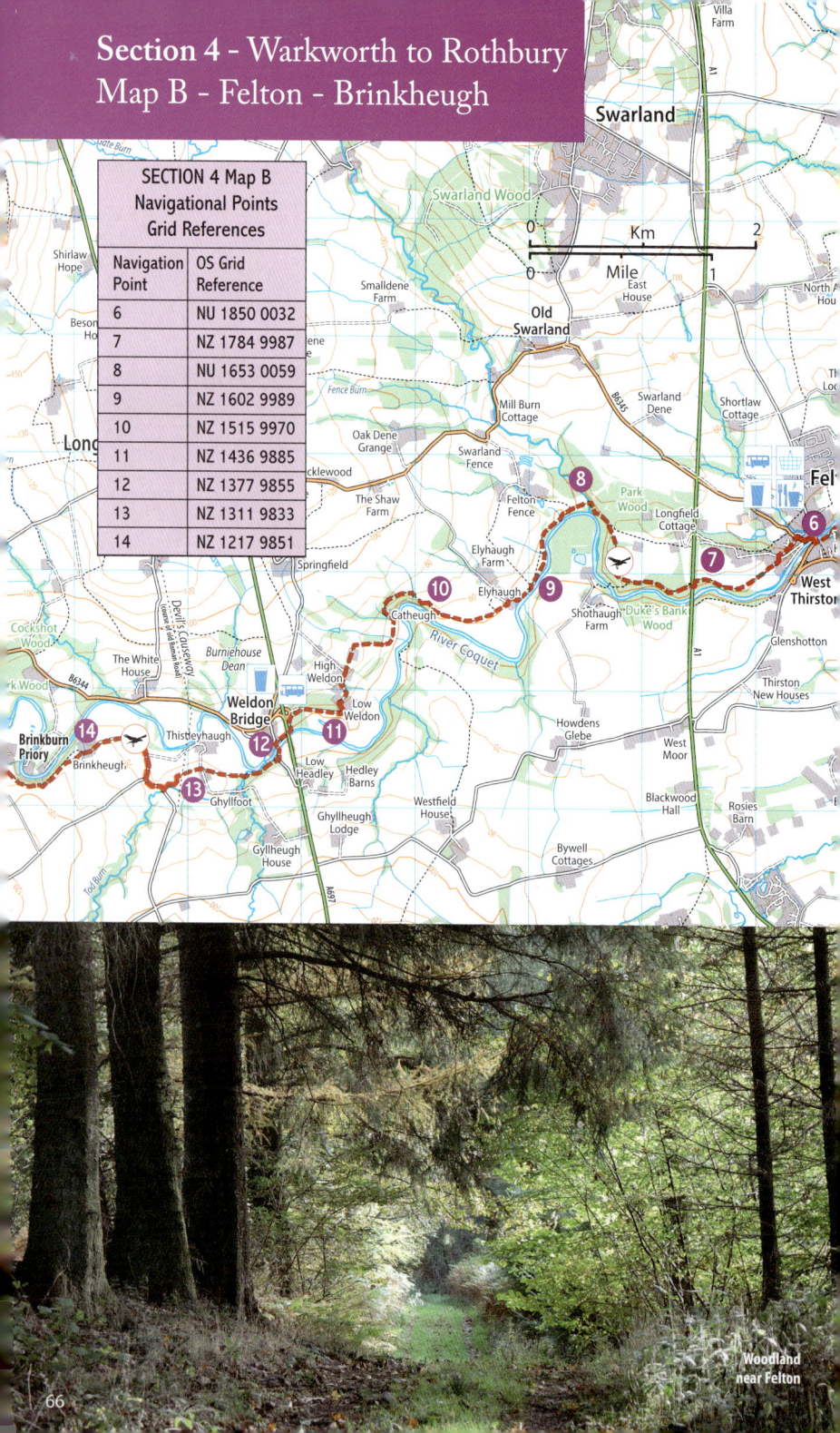

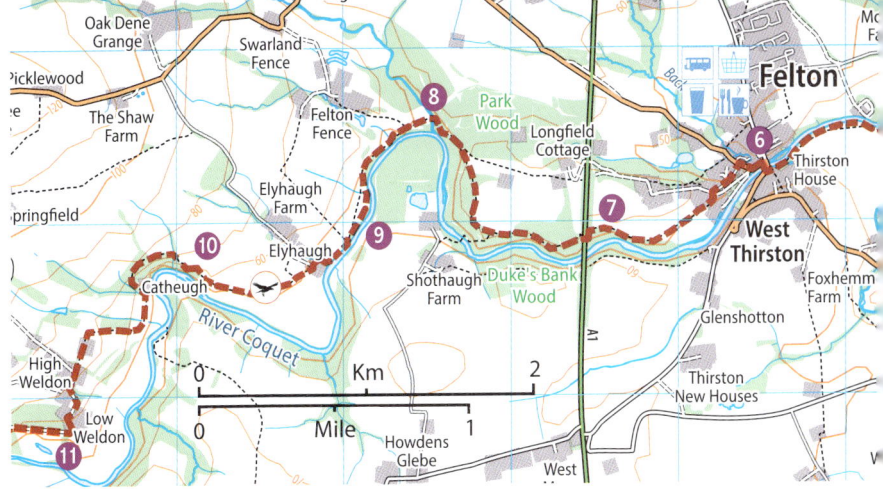

7 Pass through a gate into the edge of some woodland. Follow the path along the top of the bank, with the river down to the left through the trees. Pass under the A1 then up a flight of steps to a junction. Bear left on a woodland track and follow it ahead for ¾ mile. Bear left off the track, following the waymarked public footpath to the riverbank and along to a footbridge.

8 Cross the bridge and walk away from it, uphill. Bear left at the path junction before the top of the slope. Follow the path through the fields, parallel to the river, to reach a gate in the top corner of a field. After the gate, follow the path gradually down to the bottom edge of the field with the fence and the Coquet to your left, to reach the far corner.

9 Cross the stile in the corner of the field and walk through to a track along the riverbank. Follow the track away from the river, then turn left up the hill and around to the right of the cottage. Go through the gate and cross the parking area to another small gate. Bear right across the field to a stile. Follow the track ahead with the field boundary on your left as far as a gateway. Go straight on along the bridleway to another gate.

East of High Weldon

10 Follow the path around the edge of this field then into some woodland on the left. Head through the trees then follow the path with a hedge on your right, down to a garden. Keep to the right, down to a gate near a house (Catheugh) on the left. Follow the track up through the field and towards High Weldon. Leave the track as it turns right and go straight on along the path between the buildings. Follow the path straight on and eventually through to Low Weldon.

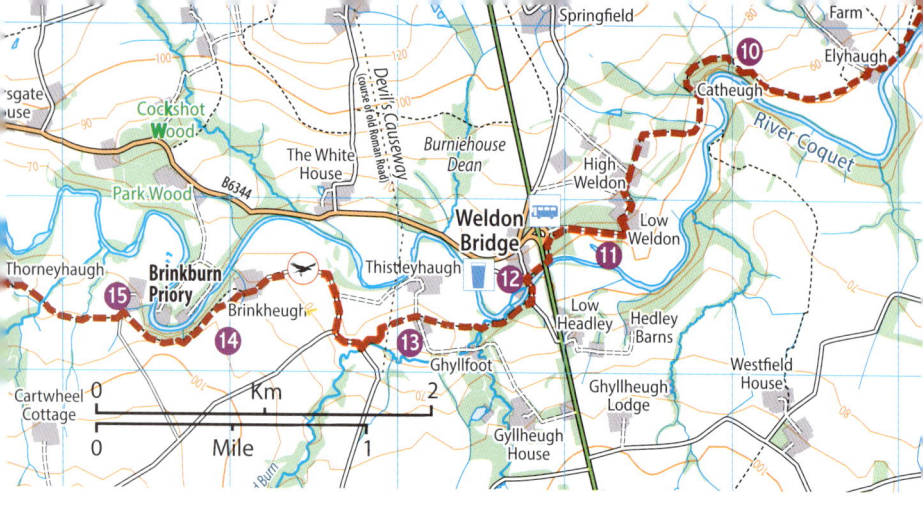

11 Pass the buildings and follow the driveway as it bends around to the right. Before the end of the driveway, bear left on a path. Follow the path under the main road and along the River Coquet, eventually reaching a road by the Anglers Arms at Weldon Bridge.

Low Weldon

12 Turn left along the road, then bear left, crossing the bridge over the river. After 100 yards, turn right on a footpath through a riverside woodland. After crossing a footbridge, follow the field edge around to the left and walk on the left-hand side of the field until reaching a second gate. Bear right, across the corner of the field, to another gate.

Anglers Arms, Weldon Bridge

13 Cross the track, then walk up the left-hand side of the field until a gate on the left. Bear left through the gate, then walk around to the right, between the bushes and down to a lane. Turn right along the lane, then bear right again at the first junction. Go straight ahead along the lane, then turn left along a stone track to reach farm buildings (Brinkheugh).

Weldon Bridge

Weldon Bridge has an unusual design, with three elliptical arches and circular openings in-between. It was built in the 18th century and replaced two earlier ones – built in 1744 and 1752 – that had been swept away by floods. The Angler's Arms was a coaching inn on the old turnpike road from Morpeth to Cornhill-on-Tweed. It is an 18th century building with a large south-west wing added in the early part of the 19th century.

14 Keep to the left of the sheds and barns then pass the farmhouse to reach a gate. Follow the waymarked path ahead, keeping to the right-hand side of fields. Through the woodland to your right, you can catch glimpses of Brinkburn Priory across the river. Follow the path around to the right and continue to walk with the woodland on your right-hand side, eventually reaching the farm of Middleheugh.

Brinkheugh

Brinkburn Priory

A loop in the river provides the setting for Brinkburn Priory on the opposite bank from the path. The Priory was founded around 1135 by William Bertram I, Baron of Mitford for Augustinian canons: these were ordained monks and, since they wore a black habit, were known as Black Canons. They did not lead a solitary life but also had pastoral duties: for example, during the Priory's existence, the vicar of Felton was a canon of Brinkburn. All that survives today of the Priory is the church, a fine late Norman building dating from 1190 - 1220 that was carefully restored in 1858.

The other main building on the site is the Manor House. After the dissolution of the monasteries, some of the buildings, probably little altered, were used as a house by George Fenwick. Although there are some 13th century remains in the basement, the building standing today was built in 1810 and extensively extended to the west in 1830-7. Last inhabited in 1952, the building was almost destroyed by extensive dry rot. Only the ground floor and some of the basement can be visited.

Both buildings are in the care of English Heritage but it is not, unfortunately, possible to visit Brinkburn directly from St. Oswald's Way.

The Devil's Causeway

The Devil's Causeway, the course of which is crossed to the west of Weldon Bridge, is the major Roman road that runs south-west across Northumberland, from the mouth of the River Tweed at Berwick to meet Dere Street (the Roman York to Edinburgh road) just to the north of Portgate on Hadrian's Wall. It is possible that Oswald and his army followed the Devil's Causeway southwards to reach Heavenfield.

Brinkburn Priory

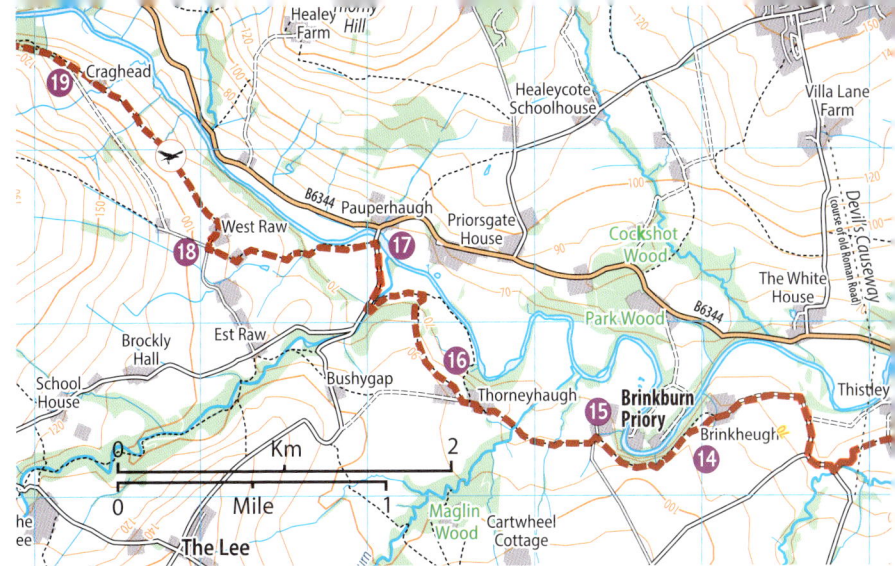

15 Cross the track near the entrance to the farmstead and follow the footpath. After a small gate, bear slightly left across the next field to a gate and stile. Go over the stile, cross the field towards the corner of a wood then go down the bank to a footbridge. Head up the opposite bank and bear left towards the far corner of the field. Go through the gate and pass to the left of Thorneyhaugh farmhouse and buildings, then go straight on along the track.

16 Just before a cattle grid, go through a gate and bear right to the far corner of the field. Walk along the right-hand side of the next field. Follow the path through the fields, with excellent views of the Coquet valley and of the Simonside Hills to your left. The path leads eventually down to a stile by the ruin of Longhaugh. Turn left after the stile and walk along the edge of the field. Follow the path ahead through the next field to a gate and footbridge on your right. Cross the footbridge then turn right along the road until just before Pauperhaugh Bridge.

17 Turn left through the gate and cross the field towards the far right-hand corner. Walk along the riverside path through the next field then turn left to reach the woodland. Go through the gate and head up the path through the trees. Enter a field then bear left around the top of a bank to meet a fence. Turn right and walk with the fence on your left until passing an old cottage. Turn right and follow the main path to a gate. After the gate, turn right onto a lane.

River Coquet at Pauperhaugh

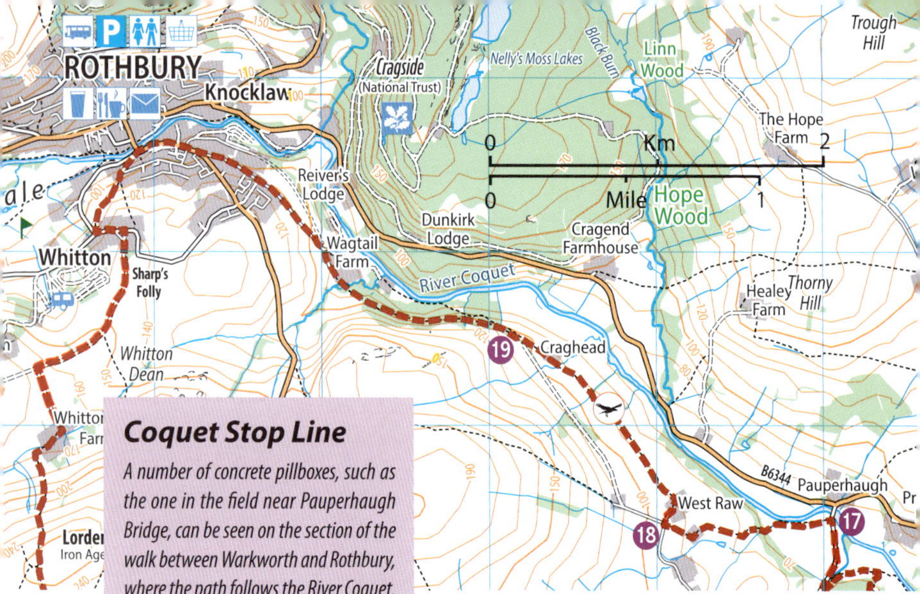

Coquet Stop Line

A number of concrete pillboxes, such as the one in the field near Pauperhaugh Bridge, can be seen on the section of the walk between Warkworth and Rothbury, where the path follows the River Coquet. These are all part of the Coquet Stop Line, one of the defence lines constructed in the early years of World War 2 to slow down any enemy advance, should a coastal landing have been successful. Making use of the natural barrier of the river, the pillboxes provided protection for soldiers defending bridges and other potential crossing places.

Pillbox at Pauperhaugh

Near West Raw

18 Go through the gateway towards West Raw. Follow the track to the left of the buildings then around to the left and ahead through the fields. The track turns into a path and eventually passes the ruined cottage of Craghead. After the building, bear left towards a gate and stile.

19 Cross onto a disused railway line and head along it to your right. Pass Wagtail Farm on your right then, after passing the remains of an old bridge, bear left along a lane. From this lane, on the other side of the valley, the Cragside Estate can be seen. Follow the lane until meeting a road, then head down the hill into Rothbury. St. Oswald's Way doesn't go into the centre of the village, which can be reached by crossing one of the bridges over the river.

Rothbury Bridge

The bridge at Rothbury probably dates from the 15th century. It was originally a three-arched packhorse bridge and a fourth arch was added at a later date. The bridge became more important when the former toll road from Hexham to the port of Alnmouth passed over it.

Rothbury Bridge

The Northumberland Central Railway

The former railway is the Northumberland Central Railway from Scots Gap to Rothbury. It was opened in 1870 and was originally conceived as an alternative route to Scotland. However it was only a single track and never went further than Rothbury. It linked to the Wansbeck Valley Railway at Scots Gap. Both companies were to become part of the North British Railway. Passenger services ceased in September 1952 and the last goods train ran on the line in 1963.

Railway cutting near Rothbury

Cragside

Lord William Armstrong, the inventor, shipbuilder and armaments manufacturer visited Rothbury regularly as a child. He came to Cragside in 1863 and had a house built there as a country retreat from his home and factories on Tyneside. From 1869, that house was vastly extended and changed into a dramatic Victorian mansion. It was the first house in the world to be lit by hydroelectricity. Several lakes were built on the estate to provide water power.

The grounds were eventually extended to 1,700 acres and were transformed from a bare-looking Northumbrian hillside into an amazing pleasure garden with a six miles long carriage drive and some 40 miles of paths. It has been suggested that seven million shrubs and trees were planted on the estate. Huge amounts of earth and rocks were moved to create rock gardens, lakes and streams. Cragside house and much of the estate are now owned by the National Trust.

Cragside

73

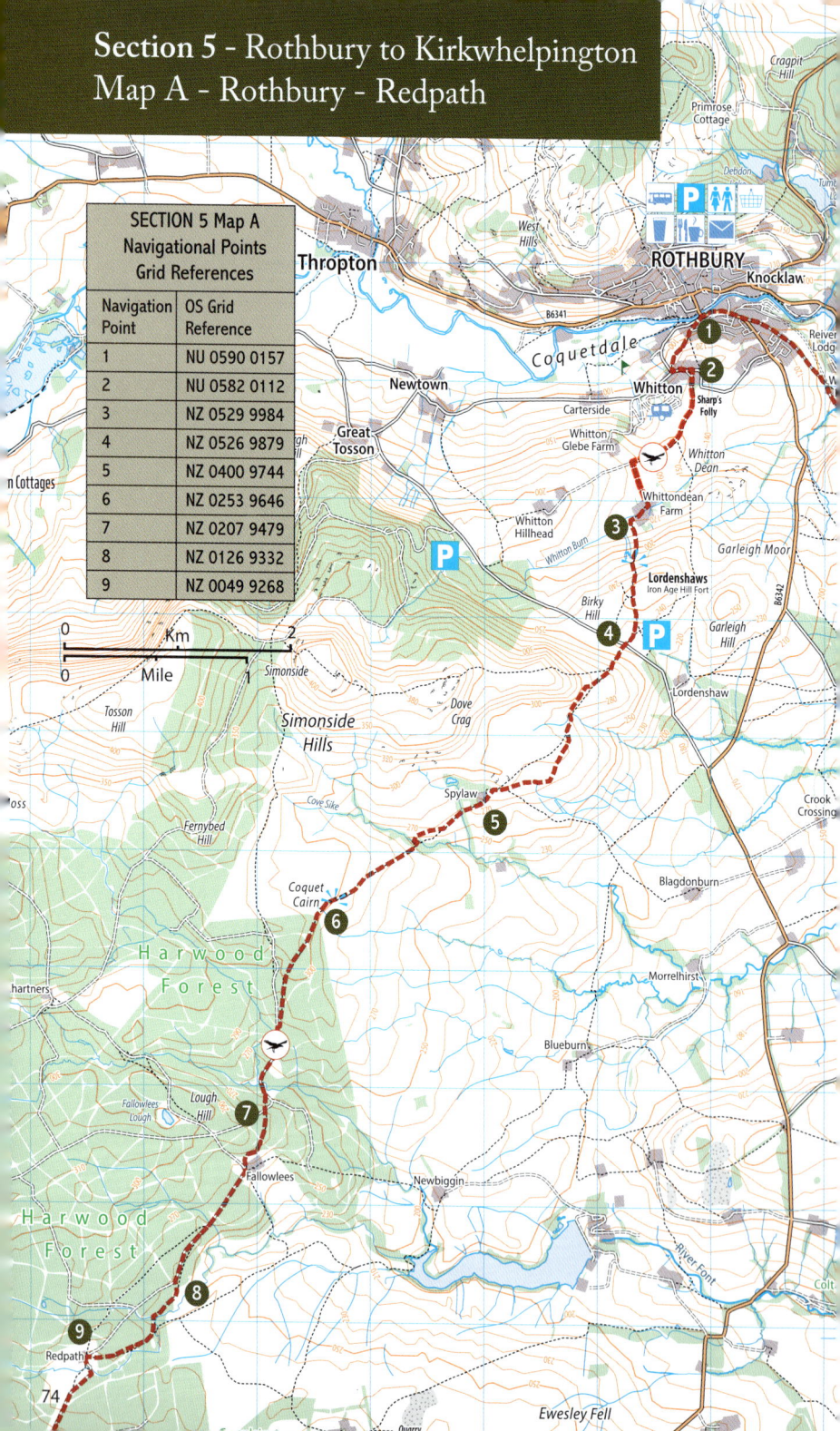

Section 5 - Rothbury to Kirkwhelpington

Rothbury

The earliest settlers in the Rothbury area left their mark locally both in the 'cup and ring' markings on stones at Lordenshaws and in many neolithic graves, especially on the Simonside Hills. The later Celtic inhabitants dwelt mainly in the hill forts that were built on many local summits. Although defeated by the Romans, they were never really assimilated and remained faithful to their former way of life.

Rothbury was probably founded early in the Anglo-Saxon era – i.e. some time after 547, when King Ida first invaded Northumberland and set up his capital at Bamburgh. The name "Rothbury" is thought to derive from a local Anglo-Saxon chieftain's personal name, meaning "Hrotha's town". It is suggested that Hrotha controlled quite a large slice of territory, with Rothbury at its centre as there are two other places, Rothley and Rothill, in the area.

All Saints Church

The earliest relic of the old town is the remains of a fine old Anglo-Saxon cross dating back to about 800, part of which can still be seen in the All Saints Church; the remainder is now in the Museum of Antiquities, in Newcastle. The church stands on the site of a much earlier Anglo-Saxon building but was rebuilt in the 13th century and extensively altered in 1850, though some 13th century work can still be seen.

Rothbury gradually became an important local market town, gaining its Charter in 1291. It suffered greatly, however, during the wars between England and Scotland and a castle was built on "Haw Hill", close to the church. Unfortunately, its remains were demolished to make way for an extension to the churchyard in 1869.

Rothbury market cross

Peace gradually returned but a period of economic decline also seems to have reduced the town to a very low ebb. Various factors helped Rothbury to recover, including the coming of the railway in 1870, which lead to the opening of an important cattle market and also encouraging the development of the town as a tourist 'health resort'. Lord Armstrong, the wealthy Victorian industrialist also poured money into the redevelopment of the town, giving it the smart Victorian appearance that it still retains today. Rothbury's market cross was erected in his honour in 1902.

Rothbury in Spring

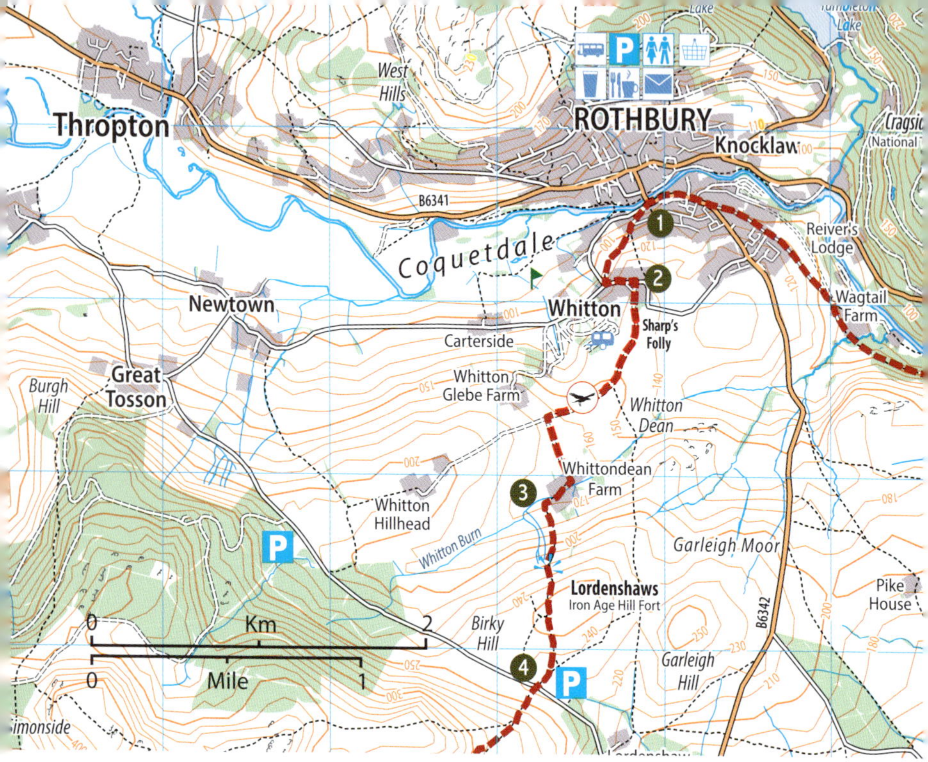

St. Oswald's Way leaves Rothbury at the end of Rothbury Bridge, across the river from the centre of the village.

1 At the bridge, head uphill on the small lane away from the river. At the top of the slope, head straight on then go through a gate into a field. Bear right on the path across and up the field to meet a road junction. Turn left at the road and head into the small settlement of Whitton

The path to Whitton

Left: **English Longhorn cattle near Rothbury**

Above: **Near Rothbury**

2 Turn off along the second track to the right. Follow the track past Sharp's Folly and onwards for another ½ mile. Turn left at the track junction and head along to Whittondean. Pass to the right of the farmhouse, then turn right along the track. Shortly afterwards, turn right off the track and follow the waymarked path through to a gate and stile.

3 The path enters rough, hilly ground and also Northumberland National Park at this point. Follow the path uphill to the fascinating archaeological site of Lordenshaws. From the hill there are superb views of the Simonside Hills, the Coquet valley, the distant Cheviot Hills and back towards the coast. An example of cup and ring-marked rocks can be seen over to the right of the main path. Follow the path ahead and downhill to Lordenshaws car park.

Sharp's Folly

4 From the car park, cross the road to the footpath opposite. Follow the path uphill, ignoring paths to the right that head towards The Beacon and the other Simonside Hills. Continue along the waymarked path across the moors and Caudhole Moss. After reaching the tree plantation, go through a gate and follow the path around to the left of Spylaw Cottage.

Sharp's Folly

Sharp's Folly was built in around 1720 by the then Vicar of Rothbury, Archdeacon Sharp, in the grounds of Whitton Park. It is said to have been built to help overcome local unemployment – an early job-creation project. However, it was also an observatory for the use of the Archdeacon who had an interest in astronomy.

Rothbury from Lordenshaws

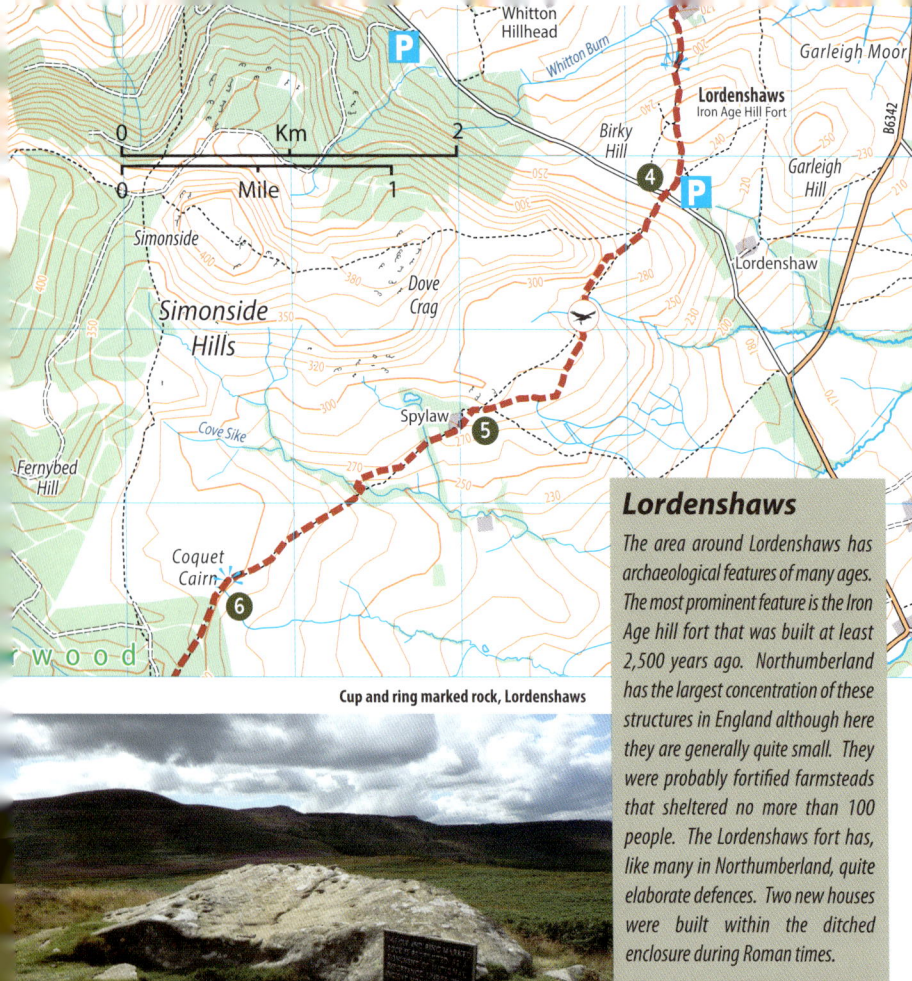

Cup and ring marked rock, Lordenshaws

Lordenshaws

The area around Lordenshaws has archaeological features of many ages. The most prominent feature is the Iron Age hill fort that was built at least 2,500 years ago. Northumberland has the largest concentration of these structures in England although here they are generally quite small. They were probably fortified farmsteads that sheltered no more than 100 people. The Lordenshaws fort has, like many in Northumberland, quite elaborate defences. Two new houses were built within the ditched enclosure during Roman times.

Of an earlier date are the 'cup and ring' marks. These are ancient carvings of the Neolithic period and possibly as much as 5,000 years old. They can be found at a number of sites throughout Northumberland and usually take the form of a cup-shaped depression surrounded by circles and grooves. The meaning of this rock art is a matter for speculation. Many of them are to be found carved on stones that command views over a wide area. This is the case with the Lordenshaws carvings, which are among the best to be found.

5 The footpath then runs across rough grazing land and more moorland to reach a footbridge across Forest Burn. Follow the track away from the Burn, with the Simonside Hills behind you. The route then continues along a footpath crossing the moor, rising slowly uphill towards a large conifer plantation. You eventually reach Coquet Cairn (the highest point of St. Oswald's Way at 1,001 ft / 305m) with good views of hills, moorland and, on a clear day, back to the North Sea.

Simonside Hills

The Simonside Hills are designated as a Site of Special Scientific Interest (SSSI) and a Special Area of Conservation (SAC) highlighting the area as both nationally and internationally important for wildlife. This area is important for the heather moorland and blanket bog habitats that are found here.

Heather moorland has developed over time as a result of human activity. Areas of woodland were gradually cleared over thousands of years for timber and to allow grazing of stock. Grazing prevents tree regrowth and extensive areas of dwarf shrub (heathers, bilberry etc.) develop. Heather burning or cutting provides fresh shoots for sheep and grouse to eat and maintains areas of varied length heather.

Cheviot Hills from Simonside

Blanket bog, such as Caudhole Moss, forms where conditions are cool and wet and where bog mosses (sphagnum) and other bog plants flourish. When the sphagnum moss dies, the waterlogged conditions mean they don't break down fully and remain partially decomposed and build up to form peat. These layers of peat build up over time and in places on the Simonside Hills may exceed 15 metres in depth. Healthy peat bogs capture and store large amounts of carbon so reduce climate change, but this can be lost when the bog is damaged or drained.

Simonside Hills

Species that may be seen include red grouse, roe deer, skylarks, meadow pipits, wheatears, sphagnum, heather (both ling and bell heather), bilberry, crowberry and bog plants such as cotton grass, bog asphodel and sundews. Rarer species that may be found in the area include red squirrels in the conifer blocks and ravens and peregrines around the crags. Ravens were once heavily persecuted as pests on farmland and game estates, but protection has helped their numbers to recover. They are large and very intelligent birds and, if you look up, you may see them soaring and tumbling high above.

6 Go through the gate to the right of the cairn and enter Harwood Forest. This is a working forest and subject to large-scale operations such as tree felling and planting. Conditions are liable to change and navigation can be difficult, so follow all signage. Follow the path ahead, bear left at a junction and continue until reaching a stone forestry track. Turn left and follow the track for ¼ mile. After crossing a bridge, walk uphill for a short distance, then leave the track on a path to the right. Walk up the path, cross the stone track and go straight ahead into a plantation.

Coquet Cairn, highest point on St Oswald's Way

Harwood Forest

Harwood Forest, planted predominantly in the 1950s by the Forestry Commission is a 3,500 hectares (13½ square miles) woodland. The original crop was planted to provide a strategic reserve for the country following the Second World War. Since the 1990s the forest has started to see a lot of changes with a number of areas being felled. The uneven age structure that is created provides a diverse habitat for a wide variety of wildlife and also allows distant views both within and to the outside of the woodland.

The areas close to the streams are also being managed to create open broadleaf woodland. This creates an ideal habitat for encouraging the passage of wild animals through the area. While walking through keep a look out for roe deer, red squirrels, raptors, crossbills, siskins and many smaller songbirds. The forest is one of northern England's red squirrel reserves.

This is a working forest so keep a look out for current activities and observe all warning signs.

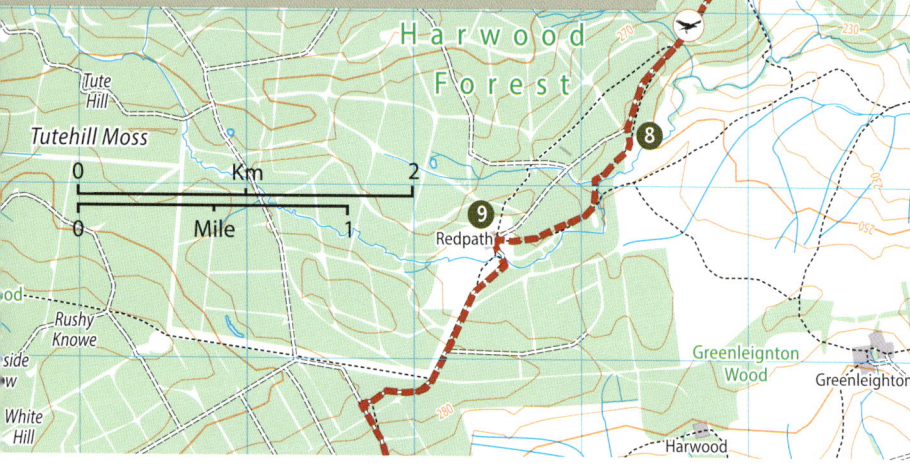

7 Follow the narrow path through the trees until you reach a dry stone wall. Turn right and follow the path along the wall, through two gates and across to a forestry track. Turn left towards Fallowlees farmhouse, then follow the track around to the right. Continue along the track for ¾ mile then, on a right-hand bend, bear left onto a small footpath.

Fallowlees

Looking east towards Fontburn Reservoir from Harwood Forest

8 Follow the path to a stile shortly afterwards and bear right across the corner of a field to a second stile. Follow the path ahead through the rough ground. Turn left to cross a stream and up the bank to pass the remains of a small building. Continue along a wide path for about 400 yards, before bearing right up a bank onto a narrow path. Follow the rough path (waymarked as a bridleway) gradually uphill then down to a gate. Cross the rough field to the old farmhouse of Redpath.

9 Turn left along the forestry track, past the open fields and back into the forest. When reaching a T-junction, turn left and follow the track down into the small settlement of Harwood.

Redpath

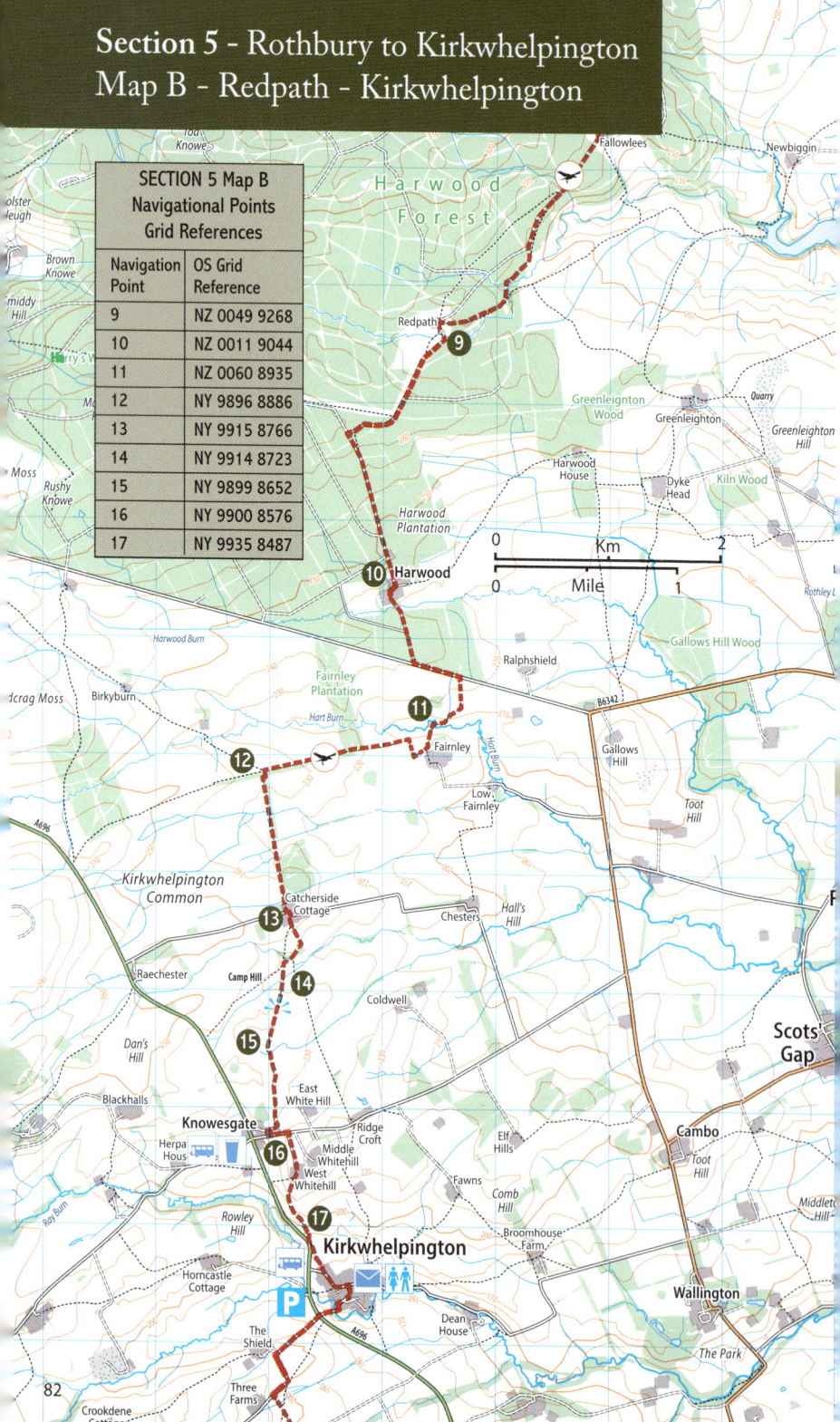

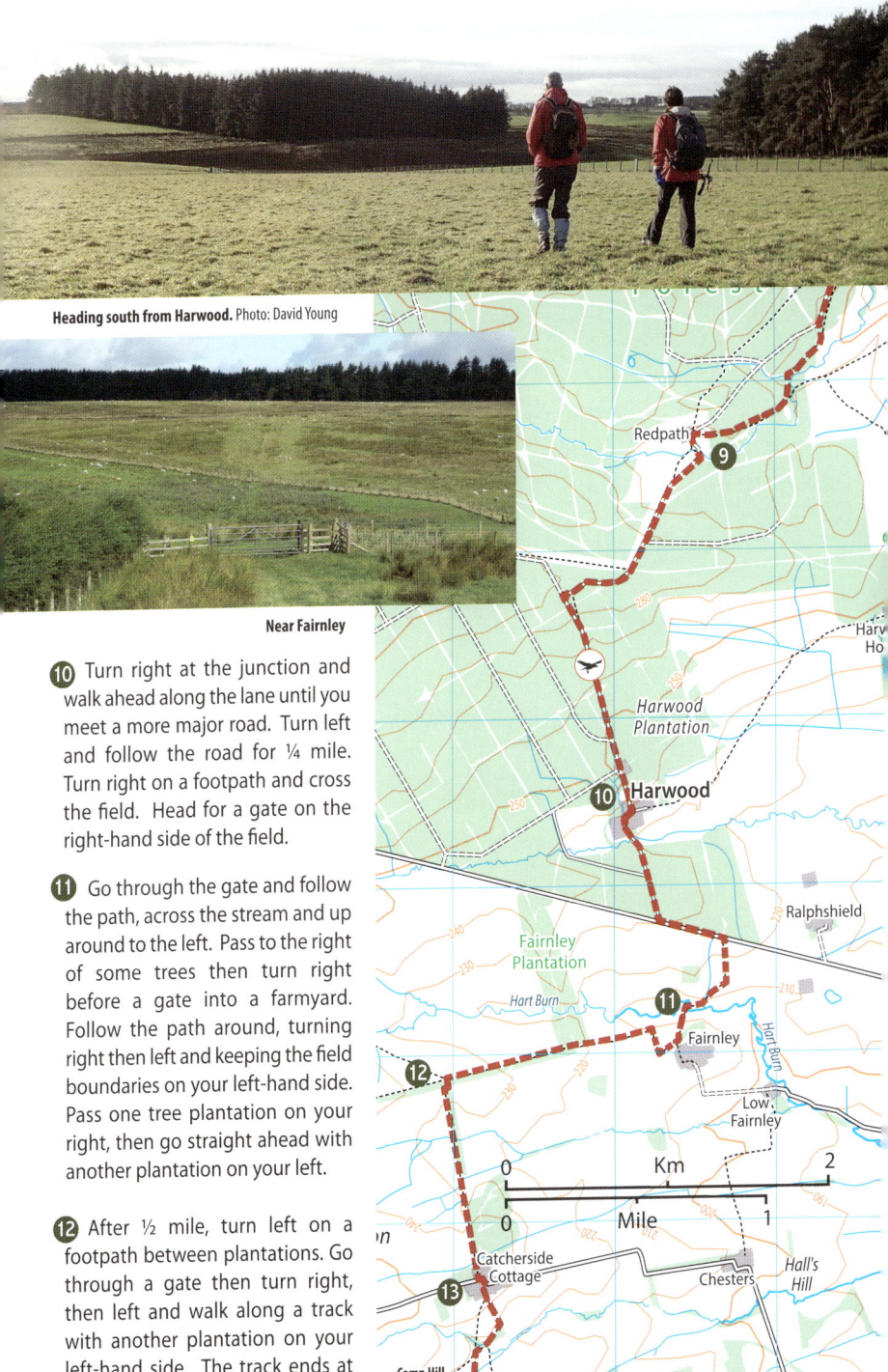

Heading south from Harwood. Photo: David Young

Near Fairnley

10 Turn right at the junction and walk ahead along the lane until you meet a more major road. Turn left and follow the road for ¼ mile. Turn right on a footpath and cross the field. Head for a gate on the right-hand side of the field.

11 Go through the gate and follow the path, across the stream and up around to the left. Pass to the right of some trees then turn right before a gate into a farmyard. Follow the path around, turning right then left and keeping the field boundaries on your left-hand side. Pass one tree plantation on your right, then go straight ahead with another plantation on your left.

12 After ½ mile, turn left on a footpath between plantations. Go through a gate then turn right, then left and walk along a track with another plantation on your left-hand side. The track ends at the farm of Catcherside.

Catcherside Cottage
Photo: David Young

Catcherside

Catcherside Cottage is, in origin, a bastle probably built in the late 16th century. Bastles were rectangular, defensible houses with a barn below and living accommodation above, and were built with three-feet thick walls. This design helped protect a family and their livestock from the border raiders or 'reivers' who were common at the time. The building was altered to a cottage in the early 19th century.

Near Catcherside

13 Turn left at the end and follow the roadway around to the right and through a gateway towards the farmhouse. Before the farmhouse, turn left on the bridleway and go through the right-hand of the two gateways. Follow the bridleway straight ahead and along the left-hand edge of the field. Bear right at the end of the field and follow the boundary to a gate. Follow the path through to another gateway.

14 When entering the next field, bear left on a public footpath, with Camp Hill to your right. Go across the field, pass through a rough, fenced area, then head to the top of the small hill to reach a stile in the far corner of the field, with lovely all-round views of a typical Northumbrian landscape. Cross the next field to another stile.

Camp Hill

Between 2000 and 3000 years ago, during the Iron Age, people lived in the defended settlement or hillfort at Camp Hill, surrounded by a ditch and rampart. 'Cord rig' earthworks can be seen outside the settlement. Cord rig is a series of narrow ridges generally less than a metre apart, formed as a result of cultivation in the pre-Roman Iron Age.

Former station at Knowesgate

15 Bear left across the next field and follow the path, through a gap in a wall and around to the left of a conifer plantation. After going through a gate onto a track, turn right (parallel to an old railway), then left between the houses to meet the road at the settlement of Knowesgate.

16 Turn left and walk along the road for 200 yards, then turn right up the driveway to West Whitehill. Pass the farmhouse and follow the bridleway through some gates. Follow the line of earthworks down through the field, with a bank then an old dry stone wall on your left. There are views, on a clear day, of the distant Pennine Hills. At the bottom of the field, go through a gate on the right-hand side, onto the road verge.

17 Walk along the verge for a few yards, then leave the road at a gate on the left-hand side. Follow the path straight ahead to the edge of Kirkwhelpington. Go straight on at the road, around to the left, then turn right to the centre of the village and the Memorial Hall.

Wansbeck Valley Railway

The Wansbeck Valley Railway (known locally as 'The Wannie Line') was built between 1862 and 1865. It ran from Morpeth to Redesdale, where it joined the Border County Railway line from Hexham to Hawick. There was a station at Knowesgate, which is now a private house just to the left of the path.

Near Kirkwhelpington

Earthworks north of Kirkwhelpington

Between West Whitehill and the village of Kirkwhelpington, there are a number of ridges and hollows in the fields. These have been made in a variety of ways, including for a medieval field system. There are also a series of 'hollow ways' that appear to lead towards the village. They have steep sides and are thought to have been created by the movement of packhorses and livestock. They were probably part of a droving route between England and Scotland.

Kirkwhelpington St Bartholomew's Church

Kirkwhelpington

The name 'Whelpington' begins to appear in documents in the mediaeval period. During this time there was a village at West Whelpington, which had at least 25 houses. The tenants were all evicted in 1720 in the name of more modern agricultural practices. The remains of the village are perched on the edge of a former whinstone quarry.

The present St. Bartholomew's church in Kirkwhelpington was built in the 13th century, with the first recorded vicar being Walter Crespyn in 1244. It was originally a larger building, with aisles and transepts.

The parish took a long time to recover from the border troubles during the 16th and 17th centuries. Restoration work was carried out on the church during the 18th century and the oldest gravestones in the churchyard date from this time. One of the most interesting modern graves is that of Sir Charles Parsons (1854-1931), the inventor of the steam turbine, who lived nearby. In 1760 the Vicar's tower or pele was altered and extended. The Rev. John Hodgson lived here between 1823 and 1832 when he wrote most of his classic 'History of Northumberland'.

The rest of the village was made of simple, heather-thatched, two-roomed dwellings until the 1850s, when the stone built, slate roofed cottages, which now characterise the village began to be built. Many of the purpose-built buildings are now private dwellings. The grey stone Court House was built in 1851 with the large courtroom taking up the first floor and the policeman's house and prison cells on the ground floor. The school was built in 1858 by public subscription but closed in 1972. Overlooking the village green was 'The Board Inn'. After a petition by wives of the village in 1916, the inn was changed to a 'temperance hotel'. The old blacksmith's house and smithy are at the end of the village green.

Kirkwhelpington village

The bridge over the River Wansbeck was erected by voluntary subscription and labour in 1818. The date on the bridge was moved to the outside during later repair work.

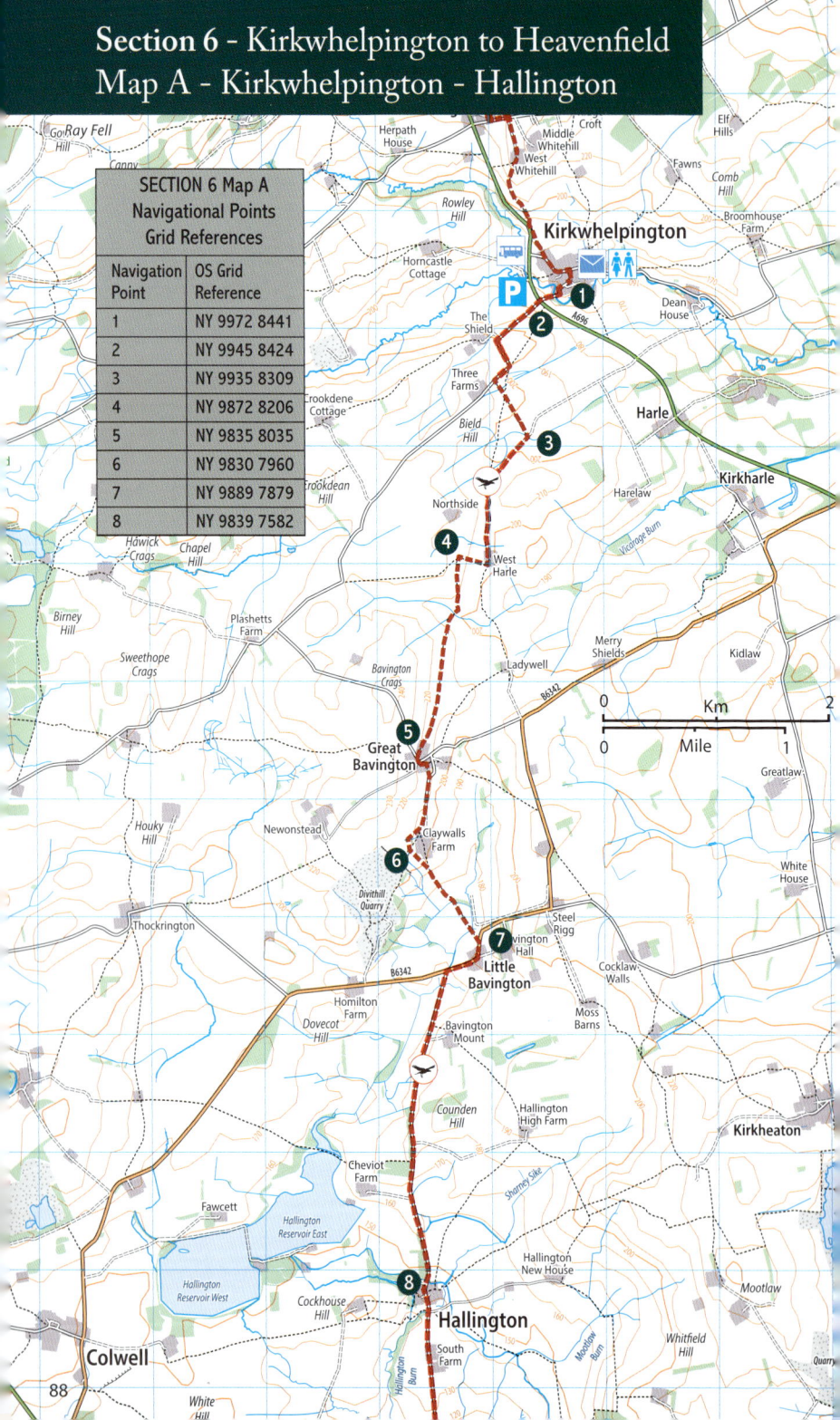

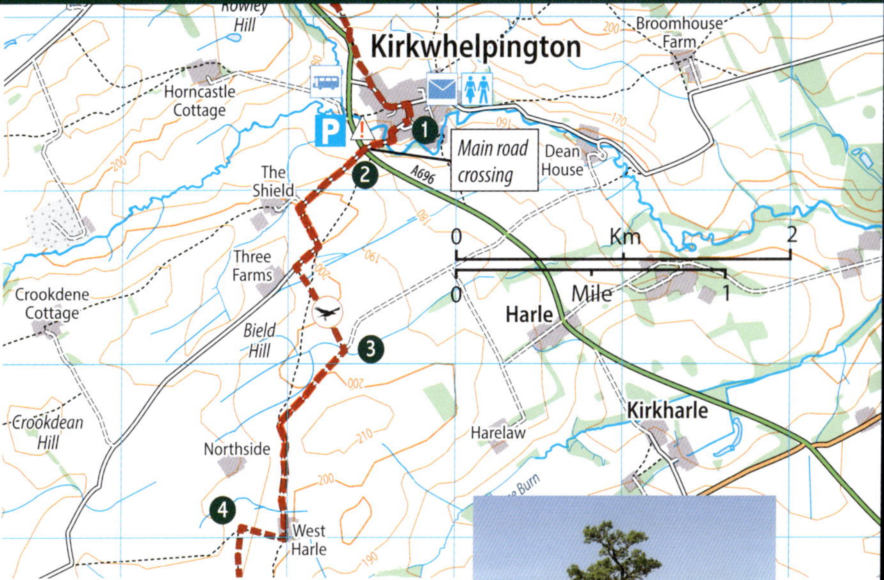

Section 6 - Kirkwhelpington to Heavenfield

1 From the Memorial Hall at Kirkwhelpington, follow the road between the Church of St. Bartholomew and the village green. Cross the River Wansbeck and meet the A696.

2 Carefully cross the main road and go straight ahead along a narrow lane. Follow the road as it bends to the left then the right, then turn left on the path just before the farm buildings. Go straight on along the path, crossing the field to meet another lane.

3 Turn right and follow the lane, ignoring the turn-off to the right, to reach West Harle. Pass the farm buildings to your left, then turn right along an old track and follow it for 300 yards.

4 Turn left through a gate then walk with the field boundary on your left. Bear right at the bottom of the field and cross a stile. Follow the path ahead towards some of the Bavington Crags, then bear left up the hill to another stile. Go straight on with the fence on your left until you reach a track and follow it ahead, to reach the small village of Great Bavington.

Top: **The Shield**

Bottom: **Near West Harle**

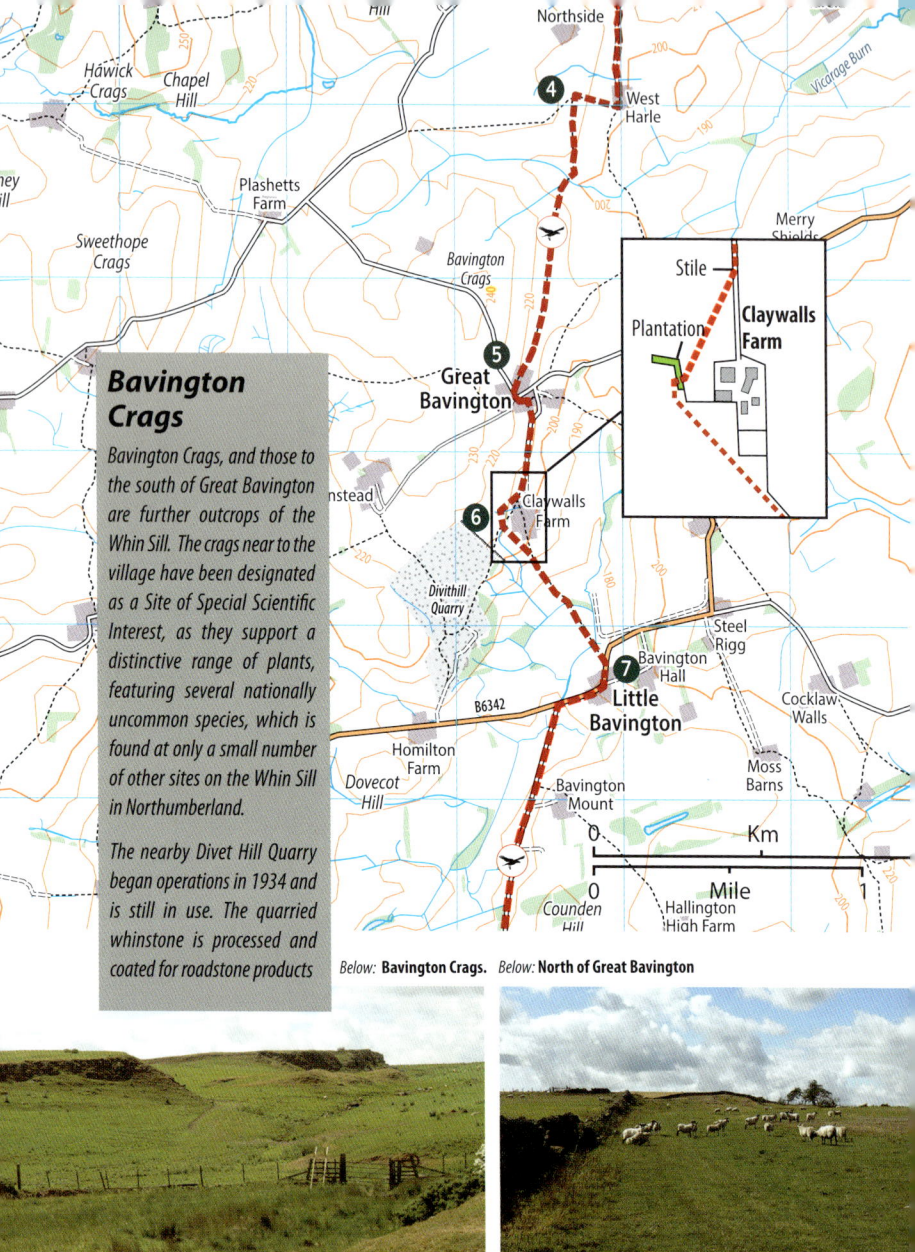

Bavington Crags

Bavington Crags, and those to the south of Great Bavington are further outcrops of the Whin Sill. The crags near to the village have been designated as a Site of Special Scientific Interest, as they support a distinctive range of plants, featuring several nationally uncommon species, which is found at only a small number of other sites on the Whin Sill in Northumberland.

The nearby Divet Hill Quarry began operations in 1934 and is still in use. The quarried whinstone is processed and coated for roadstone products

Below: **Bavington Crags.** *Below:* **North of Great Bavington**

5 After joining the road in the village, bear left onto an old track that runs between then behind houses (the Whin Sill is exposed in the surface) and around to the right past the United Reformed Church. Follow the route through to meet a driveway that leads towards a farm. About 200 yards before the buildings, bear right over a stile and across a field. Cross the next two stiles and follow the path through a small plantation.

❻ Turn left after the plantation then follow the waymarked path to the right of the farmhouse, past a field corner, then down the field on the right-hand side of an old dry stone wall. At the bottom of the field, bear right through a gate and past a small plantation, then bear slightly left across the next field to a small bridge and gate. Go straight ahead along a line of trees to reach the road in Little Bavington.

Near Claywalls

❼ Cross the road when safe to do so and turn right, walking around the outside of the sharp right-hand bend ahead. About 200 yards after the bend, turn left along a lane. Dovecot Hill can be seen to the right from this lane. Continue straight on to eventually reach the small settlement of Hallington.

Great Bavington

Although it is now a very small, quiet village built on the Whin Sill, Great Bavington used to be much larger and has existed for at least a thousand years. The village probably reduced in size due to outbreaks of the plague and poor harvests in the 14th century.

The oldest building now standing in the village was built in 1625 and was once a pub called the 'Harvest Home'. Next door is what was the village school, which has a Victorian postbox in the wall. After the school closed, it became a popular youth hostel: however, this was closed due to the 'unseemly behaviour' of the hostellers.

Great Bavington

The nearby United Reformed Church was built in 1725, replacing an earlier Dissenters meeting house of the late 17th century. The Dissenters were Christians who did not accept the 1662 Act of Uniformity. The church is the second oldest Presbyterian church in England and has a sundial on its south wall.

Little Bavington

Little Bavington is another settlement with a long history. Evidence of a deserted mediaeval village has been found and there are records of a chapel in the 13th century and a possible tower in later years.

Bavington Hall, in the park to the east of Little Bavington, is a solid and sizeable stone house built in the late 17th century, probably for Admiral George Delaval. It has since been altered, extended and repaired. It used to stand in large-scale 18th century landscaped gardens although little of these now remain.

Dovecot Hill

Dovecot Hill

To the west of Little Bavington, on a small hill, is the most significant remainder of the landscaped gardens of Bavington Hall. This was built as an 'eyecatcher' and to look like a miniature castle. It may have been a dovecot as well as a focal point.

8 Continue ahead along the lane for another mile until reaching a crossroads. Cross carefully and go straight ahead past the war memorial. Follow the road around to the right at the top of the hill, then turn left onto a bridleway a little further on. Follow the bridleway ahead, along the edge of a field and up the right-hand side of a narrow plantation.

'The Cut' water supply channel, Hallington

Hallington

The four reservoirs in the Hallington area were built by the Newcastle and Gateshead Water Company to supply water to Tyneside. East Hallington, with a capacity of 685 million gallons (3.1 million cubic metres), was completed in 1872. A number of geological problems had to be overcome in the construction of the 1068 million gallon Colt Crag Reservoir which came into use in 1884. The much smaller Little Swinburn was completed in 1879 and the fourth, West Hallington, followed shortly afterwards.

Hallington Hall was built for Ralph Soulby in 1768. Alterations and additions were made in the late-18th and mid-19th centuries for the subsequent owners, the Trevelyans. A Roman altar and a dovecot stand in the grounds of the Hall.

War memorial near Hallington Mill

Section 6 - Kirkwhelpington to Heavenfield
Map B - Hallington - Stagshaw/Portgate

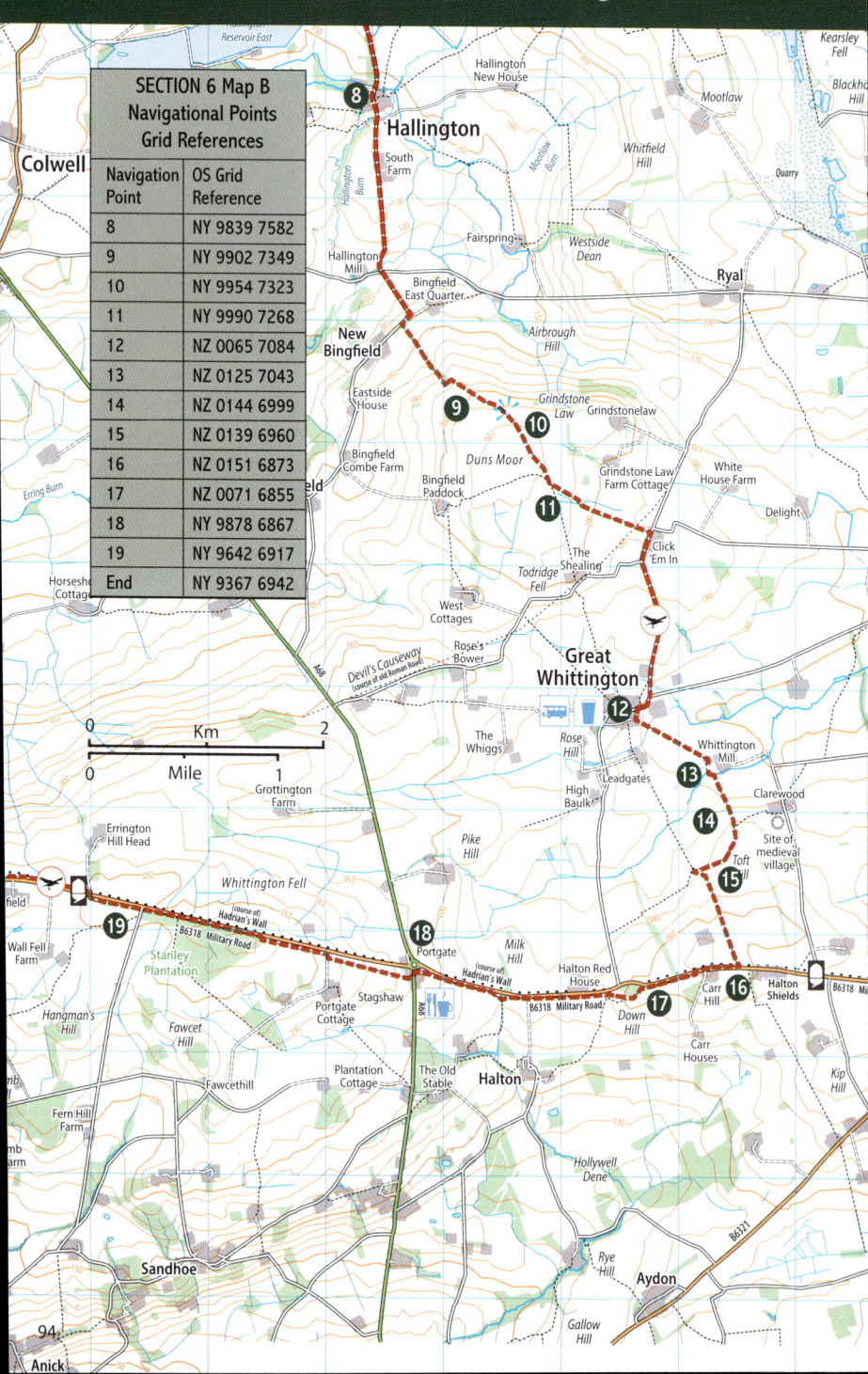

9 Go around the top of the plantation and through a small gate into a rough field. Walk uphill with a wall on your right-hand side, to a gate at the top of the field. There are excellent views to the north from this point.

10 After going through the gate, go straight ahead across the next field. At the next gate, bear left towards another gate in the far corner of the field, passing the highest point of Todridge Fell to your right. Lovely views across the Tyne valley to the Pennines can be see to the south on a clear day. Walk along the edge of the next field for about 100 yards, to a small gate on your left.

Looking north from Duns Moor

11 Go through the gate and hedge, then bear right across the field. Walk near to a fence on your right to reach another gate. Go through the gate and turn left along the edge of the field. Follow the path straight ahead, crossing the course of the Devil's Causeway, to reach the road at Click 'Em In. Turn right at the road and, ignoring roads on the right then the left, follow it through to the village of Great Whittington.

Great Whittington

Much of the village of Great Whittington, with its attractive stone houses, was built in the early 19th century. Several of the houses were formerly used for other purposes and there were a number of farmhouses in the village.

Next to the small village green is a house that was the blacksmith's forge. In the past, almost every village and town would have had a blacksmith. The blacksmith would not have actually produced the metal, but would have made or repaired smaller iron-based items.

Great Whittington also has an interesting Methodist history, including a small Wesleyan Chapel that was built in 1835 but has since been converted into a house. There was also a 'temperance' inn and hotel in the centre of the village. Methodists set up a number of hotels that did not serve alcoholic drinks as part of the Temperance Movement. This was such a building in the 19th century but is also now a house.

The tree on the village green is the 'Coronation Tree', a horse chestnut planted on the 2nd of June 1953, to celebrate the coronation of Queen Elizabeth II.

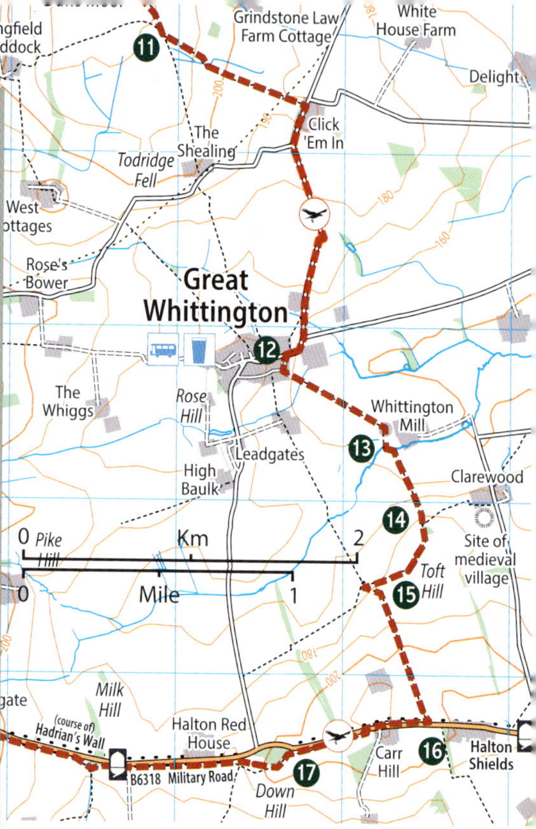

Former Wesleyan Methodist chapel, Great Whittington

12 Just before the Queen's Head, turn left onto a track. At the bend ahead, turn left through a gate, then bear left through another gate. Follow the path, crossing a ditch then straight ahead to a gate and stile. Go straight on and walk up the right-hand side of the field to an old windmill.

13 Cross the boundary at the windmill and cross the field to reach a footbridge. After the footbridge, turn left along the edge of the field. Turn right at the corner, again following the edge of the field, until reaching a gate at the far end.

14 Go straight on up to the top of the hill to the right of the trees and head for a gate in the fence in front of you. Go through the gate and bear right, down to a small gate to the right of the far corner of the field.

Whittington Mill

Whittington windmill is a round stone building and was probably constructed in the 18th century. Only the walls of the mill now survive; the sails and roof blew off in 1900. Close to the windmill is an 18th century, three-storey watermill and the west gable used to house the wheel. This site has probably been home to a watermill since mediaeval times.

15 Go through the gate and walk along the left-hand edge of the field to a small gate and then a ladder stile. Cross the stile then go through a small gate into another field. Bear left across the corner of the field, then walk along the field-edge to meet a road.

16 At the road, St. Oswald's Way joins Hadrian's Wall Path National Trail and, for the rest of the route, is waymarked with the acorn symbol used for all National Trails. Turn right and follow the path alongside the road. After Carr Hill farm, the route crosses to the other side of the road, then follows the edges of fields on the other side of a wall. In this area, some of the earthworks of Hadrian's Wall can be seen, with the Vallum in the field to the left and the North Ditch across the road to the right.

Whittington Mill

Hadrian's Wall at Planetrees west of Heavenfield

Hadrian's Wall

The Roman Emperor Hadrian visited Britain in 122 and it is thought that he ordered the Wall to be built at that time. It was built in the following six years by the Roman army, although modifications were still being carried out when Hadrian died in 138. The Wall was not essentially a defensive structure: its main purpose was frontier control, guarding the Roman Empire to the south. As first planned, there were gates every Roman mile with small guard posts (milecastles). There are the sites of five milecastles along St. Oswald's Way.

However, the Roman frontier was not just a wall. To the north there was usually a ditch to make the Wall more defensible and, to the south, an earthwork known as the Vallum. The Vallum stretched almost the whole length of the wall and was a flat-bottomed ditch (about 20 feet wide and 10 feet deep) with a mound, set back by 30 feet, on either side. Opinions vary as to the purpose of the Vallum: some historians believe it to have marked the southern side of a 'military zone' behind the Wall, while others think that it may been a communication route.

Portgate and Stagshaw

A major Roman road (now known as Dere Street) was built in around AD79/80 stretching from their important centre of York to Edinburgh. Today's A68 follows the route of Dere Street in this area. When Hadrian's Wall was built in later years, the Romans created a massive gateway, with twin gates and towers, to accommodate the road, and this stood very close to today's roundabout (known locally as the Stagshaw roundabout). It became known as Portgate, probably during the Anglo-Saxon period. Oswald and his army may well have passed through Portgate on their way to and from the Battle of Heavenfield.

Stagshaw Bank, nearby to the south of Hadrian's Wall, was once famous for its livestock fairs. Thousands of cattle, sheep and horses were brought to these markets, which attracted people from all over northern England and southern Scotland. Each fair lasted for a week or more and was a spectacular event, full of people and animals.

Stagshaw Fair was hugely important in the Middle Ages for trade in goods as well as livestock. It is thought that the fairs could have had much earlier origins, and they certainly survived for many centuries. Armstrong's map of 1769 marks Stagshaw Bank as the site of "two of the greatest fairs in England".

17 Head around the left-hand side of the trees on top of a small hill and towards the Vallum, with good views of the Tyne Valley. Cut back down to the road at a stile in the corner of the field. Follow the path, parallel to the road, until the A68 at Stagshaw/Portgate.

18 At the roundabout, head around to the left and cross the A68 to the left of the Errington Coffee House. Go through the car park and follow the path through the fields, with the Military Road over to the right.

The Vallum from Down Hill

Section 6 - Kirkwhelpington to Heavenfield
Map C - Stagshaw/Portgate - Heavenfield

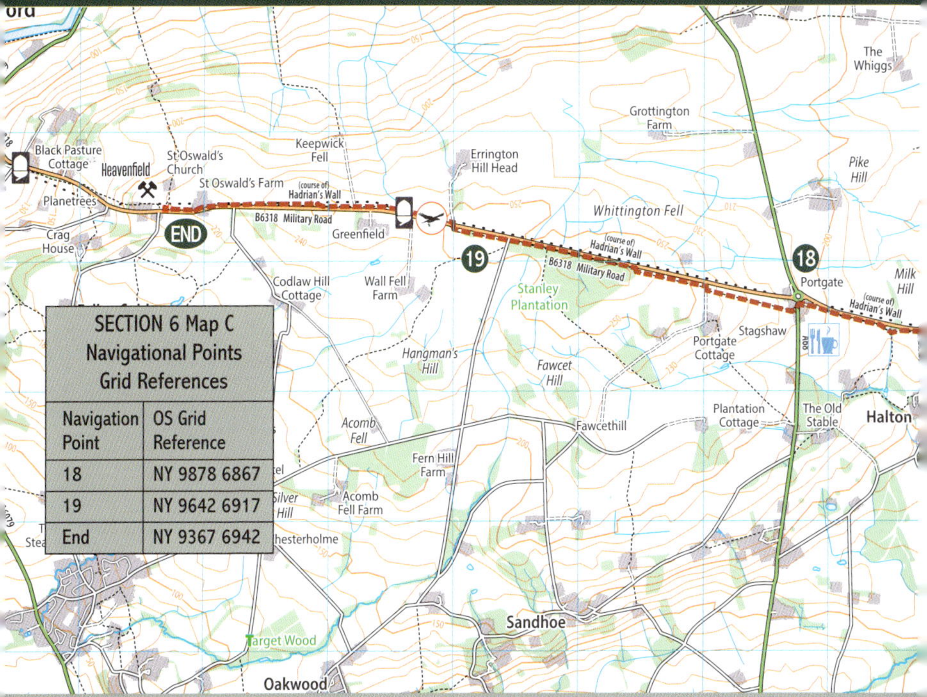

SECTION 6 Map C Navigational Points Grid References

Navigation Point	OS Grid Reference
18	NY 9878 6867
19	NY 9642 6917
End	NY 9367 6942

The Military Road

The Military Road was built in the 18th century. Its origins lay in 1745 when the English army, under Field Marshal George Wade, stationed in Newcastle, was unable to reach Carlisle to intercept the invading Scottish army led by Bonnie Prince Charlie. The poor and wet road that the English army had to follow was too near the Tyne Valley, so a new road on higher ground was the answer.

The new road is often incorrectly credited to Wade, possibly due to the similar roads he had built in earlier years in Scotland, but he died three years before construction started in 1751. Much of the Military Road was built almost exactly on the line of Hadrian's Wall and, since it used the Roman stones as a foundation, frequently on top of it. It was very controversial at the time due to the destruction of remains of the Wall.

The Military Road

19 After leaving the trees of Stanley Plantation and crossing a side-road, the route goes through more fields before crossing the Military Road again near Errington Hill Head. Cross carefully then follow the path through the fields to the right of the road. After 1¼ miles, pass St. Oswald's Farm and through to the large wooden cross at Heavenfield, the end of St. Oswald's Way. **END**

End of St. Oswald's Way, Heavenfield cross

Heading for Heavenfield

Heavenfield

St Oswald's Church, Heavenfield

Oswald's uncle, Edwin, had killed Oswald's father, King Aethelfrith to reign in Northumbria. However, in 633 he was killed in a battle against Cadwallon, the King of Gwynedd, and Penda of Mercia. For a while, Oswald's elder step-brother Eanfrith was king, until he too was killed by Cadwallon.

Oswald had returned from exile when Edwin was killed. He marched south with a small army to Heavenfield to confront Cadwallon, "the accursed leader of the Britons and all that vast army that he boasted none could resist".

The Battle of Heavenfield took place in around 634. The night before the battle, Oswald and his men were stationed here and built and erected a large wooden cross on the high ground and prayed to God for success in their fight.

The following day, Oswald and his army won an important victory. It isn't clear from historical records where the battle took place, but a large number of skulls and sword hilts have been uncovered in a field known as Mould's Close on the south side of the road. It is thought that Cadwallon himself was killed on the banks of Rowley Burn, about seven miles to the south of here.

Monks from the abbey at Hexham held an annual pilgrimage to Heavenfield and to the wooden cross. Splinters of wood from the cross were believed to be the cause of miracles and the site became so popular that a small church was built here in the late 7th century. The present St. Oswald's Church is probably the third on the site and was built in the 18th century. An annual pilgrimage from Hexham to Heavenfield is still held, on or around St. Oswald's Day (5th August).

The large wooden cross now standing at Heavenfield was erected here by a group of local people in 1927, replacing a stone cross that had stood here until 1807. The stone cross used a Roman altar as its base stone and the altar is now in St Oswald's Church.

Heavenfield to Wall or Hexham

Unfortunately there is no public transport to Heavenfield and no suitable car parking.

Therfore you are advised to continue along Hadrian's Wall path to the village of Wall or head south into Hexham

Useful Websites

St Oswald's Way: www.stoswaldsway.com
For alterations to the route since the publication of this guidebook, see the 'Route Changes' page.

Visit Northumberland:
www.visitnorthumberland.com

Northumberland County Council:
www.northumberland.gov.uk

Northumberland National Park Authority
www.northumberlandnationalpark.org.uk

Northumberland Coast National Landscape
www.northumberlandcoast-nl.org.uk

Traveline *(for public transport information)*
www.traveline.info

National Trails *(including Hadrian's Wall Path and England Coast Path)*
www.nationaltrail.co.uk

North Sea Trail
www.northseatrail.org

Holy Island Crossing Times
www.holyislandcrossingtimes.northumberland.gov.uk

Merchandise

A variety of merchandise and maps are available from the St. Oswald's Way website:
www.stoswaldsway.com and
Northern Heritage: **www.northern-heritage.co.uk**

Acknowledgements

Author / Editor: Martin Paminter

Special thanks to Peter Carter, of the Alnwick & District Local History Society, for his excellent research.

Also thanks to everyone who supplied text and information.

Maps by Richard Ross, Active Maps Ltd.

Photographs by Martin Paminter, except where stated.

Special thanks to the St Oswald's Way Management Group, their Advisory Team and their volunteer rangers for their dedication in looking after St Oswald's Way.

Thanks also to the staff of Northumberland County Council, Northumberland National Park Authority and Northumberland Coast Natural Landscape partnership for their continued help in managing the route.

Disclaimer

Information contained in this guide is deemed to be correct at the time of going to print. Every effort has been made to ensure that the information given is accurate. Where appropriate, you should check the information is still valid before making a specific journey or completing final plans. The St. Oswald's Way Management Group accepts no responsibility for loss, injury or inconvenience sustained due to the information contained in this guide. Inclusion in this guide is not a recommendation by the St. Oswald's Way Management Group.